The Life & Times of the Real Robyn Hoode

(A Journey of Discovery)

The Life & Times of the Real Robyn Hoode

(A Journey of Discovery)

Mark Olly

Winchester, UK
Washington, USA

First published by Chronos Books, 2015
Chronos Books is an imprint of John Hunt Publishing Ltd., Laurel House, Station Approach,
Alresford, Hants, SO24 9JH, UK
office1@jhpbooks.net
www.johnhuntpublishing.com

For distributor details and how to order please visit the 'Ordering' section on our website.

Text copyright: Mark Olly 2015

ISBN: 978 1 78535 059 7
Library of Congress Control Number: 2015932358

A CIP catalogue record for this book is available from the British Library.

Design: Stuart Davies

Printed and bound by CPI Group (UK) Ltd, Croydon, CR0 4YY, UK

We operate a distinctive and ethical publishing philosophy in all
areas of our business, from our global network of authors to
production and worldwide distribution.

CONTENTS

Mark Olly would like to dedicate this book to all those who still seek after the truth.

This book constitutes a modern examination and adaptation of primarily original Late Medieval source material found mainly in *'A Gest Of Robyn Hode'* and its variants, the earliest *'Garland'* collections of stories and ballads, the *'Percy Folio'*, and a host of Medieval, antiquarian & archaeological publications covering 500 years of research, most not readily available to today's public.

Thanks & Dedications

"Live pure, speak true, right wrong, follow the king."
Tennyson's summary of chivalry.

Mark Olly received much help in the preparation of this work &
would like to express his particular gratitude to the following for
their assistance: Bob Hayes for trawling the internet and keeping
the electronics running smoothly, Bryan Lomax and his team for
filming and editing the results, Colin & Margaret Bowyer for
driving round hundreds of locations over many years and
pointing stuff out, Helen Maria Carr for specific research on
King John and related topics, all musicians and re-enactors who
have supported the live action project and kept us historically
'on track' especially musical composers Ian Finney and Andy
Coffey, and all those who have supported the project by
attending talks and presentations and contributing stories of
their own, and most of all Andrea Susan Olly for 'wifely support'
through a long and often time consuming project.

1283-1285: Than litill Iohne and Robyne Hude - Waichmen were commendit gud,
In Yngilwode and Bernysdale – And usit this tyme thar travale.

1283-1285: Then little John and Robyn Hoode – (As) Watchmen were commended good,
In Inglewood and Barnsdale – And used (in) this time there (to) travel.

Andrew de Wyntoun 'Rhyming chronicle of Scotland' up to 1408 (compiled by 1420).

Introduction: Literary Archaeology

"Many talk of Robin Hood, that never shot in his bow:
And many talk of Little John, that never did him know."
(Early Proverb from 'Life & Ballads Of Robin Hood' & first written by 'Skelton' in a play for Henry VIII.)

Imagine a situation where an archaeological excavation is nearing its end. In the sides of the trench are the layers of the ages, starting with modern day at the surface and getting older the deeper below ground you go. Eventually you reach a new surface at the bottom of the trench which is the natural undisturbed earth. This is where the oldest material remains to be excavated.

Now apply this to a story. Let's say: *"Robyn Hoode pulls onto his drive in his sports car, switches off his mobile phone, grabs a musket and a kite shield from the back seat, gets out and walks into his timber 'motte and bailey' castle through the port-cullis."*

Putting these items into date order is relatively simple for an archaeologist or historian: mobile phone (Modern), driveway (Post-War), vintage sports car (Early 19th Century), flint lock musket (17th Century), port-cullis gate (14th Century), motte and bailey castle (12th Century), and kite shield (11th Century). If you were looking for a real 'medieval' Robyn Hoode you could immediately rule out the phone, driveway, car, and musket. Going further, it is unlikely that he would own a castle with a port-cullis, and the same rationale applies, even if the 'motte and bailey' were to be 'in period', as you are principally looking for a noble forester knight, leaving only the kite shield as a potentially 'original' or 'real' element in this made-up version of a modern day Robyn Hoode story.

So our process is, in simplest terms: First eliminate the most recent story elements (the 'upper layers'), secondly examine the plausibility of items which may be close to the period (the 'lower layers'), and finally look at the oldest surviving material to form a picture of the first stages of the story under examination (the 'final ground surface'). This creates a 'master story' or 'back story' from which all the writers are working and stands the greatest possibility of being true. If it were Biblical material then it could be called the 'Q' or 'Quell' (meaning 'Source') manuscript of his complete life story.

To this we could add an 'archaeological survey' of the overall 'plot' elements, similar to an overall site survey or desk-top evaluation of an archaeological site, to see if they produce a chronology 'in time' and give clues to location or 'place'. We would now have 'time and place' information to add to the life story.

Further add to this a huge element of common sense and a good knowledge of the periods in question and there is just the possibility that the truth about the real Robyn Hoode will emerge.

However at the moment the authentic elements of this story are scattered over hundreds of surviving tales and ballads spanning over nine hundred years of repetition, popular printing, tampering and embellishment.

In the past chroniclers and story tellers had a habit of re-inventing earlier material to fit the times in which they lived (which happens even today), however there was an unwritten rule that the foundational characters and well known material should always remain familiar and un-changed – a kind of 'un-spoken copyright' amongst bards and story-tellers and 'authen-ticity of story' was also expected by audiences. Messing with the basic plot, characters and story was simply not approved of. This didn't rule out additions but, at the time the story was 'performed', these would have been obvious and treated as humorous by audiences, rather like the modern story invented for this introduction.

Tradition plays a hefty part when examining the past. Things didn't change as quickly as we are used to in the modern age. In some cases it could take three or four generations for things to 'wear out' and general society to move on. The majority of the ordinary population lived at one location and rarely ventured far from home. This is seen quite clearly in the tales of Robyn Hoode who appears to be virtually trapped in a particular geographic region and made to live over an impossibly long time period due to the ancient tradition of naming the eldest son after the father, and then also that of heroic characters adopting the names of similar predecessors. Even personal names were not established in medieval times. Famous names and nick-names were frequently adopted, especially those from well known tales, and land owners often moved stories around their various land holdings which is how some Robyn Hoode stories end up down south on estates owned by the Northern Barons.

There are also two issues of date to factor in: When exactly does our source material survive from? And what internal dating evidence do we have for actual story time-periods and chronology? As far as Robyn Hoode is concerned the answers here are surprising.

Material survives from within a few hundred years of the events it claims to record, and it is relatively simple to deduce what material was 'current' at this time and, therefore, what material was 'added in' to 'modernize' the tales for new audiences. The best example of this tampering would be the later changing kings and locations applied to the more recent versions of the stories. Across the board there are far more numerous and consistent references to the same early kings in surviving tales than later ones.

The other surprise is that the various references to 'time' scattered across the earliest stories can actually be brought back together to give a linear chronology that doesn't contradict itself. In short – it almost miraculously re-creates the framework of the original complete life story now lost.

Then the next step is to move this chronology around until the 'facts' of history, as independently recorded elsewhere, line up with the story – and this is also surprisingly possible (as this book will demonstrate). So effective and concrete is the end result that this author is almost certain there once existed a complete original 13th century 'Q' manuscript *'Complete Life Of Robyn Hoode'* written shortly after his death (possibly by someone who knew his surviving family and associates) from which all early tales were later taken.

Another simple equation assists us in our discovery of time period – simple mathematics! If, for example, there were thousands of publications and individuals carrying the name 'Robyn Hoode' (or similar spelling variations) in the 15th and 16th Centuries (the 'Age of Printing'), it would be expected that this was the result of manuscripts and story-tellers of the 14th Century.

If there were hundreds of these manuscripts and individuals using variant names of 'Robyn Hoode' in the 14th Century this could only be the result of the monastic writers, bards, performers, and story tellers of the 13th Century, even more so if such material was mainly utilized by noble families as it would take even more time to 'devolve' down to the general population.

If then, there were dozens of examples of the use of the tales and name of 'Robyn Hoode' in the 13th Century, mathematics dictates that the single origin of both the story and the named individual must belong to the 12th Century, any later period can be rejected simply on the grounds that the individual and his story would not have had any time to become established or to be disseminated far and wide. This is precisely the pattern we find with Robyn Hoode and it leads us back to the early 12th Century - exactly the period in which the majority of the old tales place his life.

In modern times we also have the advantage of the widest possible research base in the history of mankind – the internet or 'World Wide Web'. This means that scant and incomplete material which would take the antiquarians of past ages a lifetime to collect is now available to trawl by electronic means in just a few days. While all relevant material is not on the internet as some remains in private libraries, that used as the basis for the generally known story is available and it is this story that principally concerns us here. However I have, where possible, also accessed private material and alternative translations and these have added rare additional details to this book. New discoveries and translations also appear quite regularly as small published articles on the internet.

So the work here represents the first ever full archaeological assessment and survey of the oldest remaining Robyn Hoode material to survive (with a special emphasis on anything before 1650), the first ever attempt to reach a workable and authentic chronology that fits known historic facts from other recognized and contemporary sources, the first ever national British geographic assessment in the light of all the facts this presents, and the first attempt to authentically 'pin down' Robyn, his associates, and his family, in the light of all that has been discovered.

I must warn the sceptics that the level of detail and consistency that this process has thrown up is very difficult to deny or disprove.

To make the process even simpler I have placed all original source texts relating directly to the life of the real Robyn Hoode in **Bold Type,** so it can be read as a complete separate narrative if desired, and all the source manuscripts and quotes are in *Italics.*

Furthermore, I would hope that literary archaeology should result in the same basic foundations being discovered in a story even if entirely new material should come to light at a later date.

It should still 'fit the picture' when the basic elements are examined. And therein lies a challenge for scholars in the future.

I have no doubt that this book will be taken apart by 'experts' and applied to various fields of specialty to test its 'validity' – but it is my hope that eye-brows are raised when they find that it is indeed possible that we have arrived at the original, underlying, ground into which the first foundations of 'The Life & Times Of The Real Robyn Hoode' were laid out all those many centuries ago.

MARK OLLY – SUMMER 2014.

Rising Mists On The Cheshire Plain.

"If any reader please to try,
As I direction show,
The truth of this brave history,
He'll find it true, I know."

'A True Tale Of Robin Hood' by Martin Parker, published 1632.

1

A Working Chronology for The Life & Times of the Real Robyn Hoode

"I kan noght parfitly my Paternoster as the preest it syngeth,
But I kan rymes of Robyn hood and Randolf Erl of Chestre."

"I do not know my paternoster (prayers) perfectly as the priest sings it,
But I know rhymes of Robin Hood and Ranulf, Earl of Chester."

Piers Plowman (spoken by 'Sloth'), William Langland C1362.

The following book represents a reconstruction of a time-line for the life and times of the real Robyn Hoode based on actual known historical events and the associations given to them by the early tales of Robyn Hoode. To this has been added a measure of geographic knowledge to create a realistic life story, with many additional elements from the earliest surviving literature about him, and archaeological notes where relevant. Attention has also been given to the development of relevant early Medieval 'orders' such as Hospitallers, Templars, Crusaders, Foresters, Yeomen, Monastic Orders, etc. and to those noble families and Northern Barons with known associations to the early tales.

My apologies if the time-line format or 'diary style' approach to organizing Robyn's life does not appeal to every reader, however there is simply so much material involved that a chronological approach, in the style of such earlier Victorian publications, is felt to be the only practical way to organize Robyn's life-story, and it should enable any future researchers to find a place in which to insert any new discoveries, or expand on their own particular area of interest.

I have chosen in preparing this chronology of the life and times of the real Robyn Hoode, not to use any sources that can not be academically traced or authenticated to before 1650 unless it is the only material available. Any later surviving sources are given less credence and prominence and are subject to even greater critical scrutiny.

The Reign Of King William II (1087-1100)

Early Medieval times could be summarized as various attempts to put stability into a highly unstable European almost 'post-tribal' society. The Crusades began this trend when a 'bored' Norman aristocracy had simply to find something to do, something worthwhile they could focus on, and they chose what they were best at – conquest! The result was the establishment of a number of Religious and Civil institutions unique to that age and ultimately of importance to the seeker of Robyn Hoode, his men, and his various opponents.

Britain was certainly not immune to these trends. King William I had not entirely succeeded in conquering every corner of a realm containing Saxons, Vikings, Danes, Picts, Scots, Irish, and Welsh, and he had particular difficulties throughout his reign with 'The North' which began in the lands above the river Trent and became established and 'hard core' north of the river Mersey. This was land formerly held by tribes like the Brigantees and Setanti who withstood the in-flux of the Roman Empire and attempts at invasion by Norwegian Vikings from the West and Danes from the east.

However, the 11th Century closed after the battle of Hastings in 1066 with the early establishment of all things traditionally

'Medieval' and with William The Conqueror attacking Chester and the north in the winter of 1072, the famous 'Harrying Of The North', during which Viking and Danish settlers were spared, Saxons were slaughtered and dispossessed, and any supporters of King Harold permanently removed (a process most graphically shown by the names and value of lands held in the 'Domesday Survey').

A fairly reliable story places King Harold at St John's Church in Chester having escaped Hastings and living as a hermit with an injured left leg (an injury shown on the Bayeux Tapestry). He is said to have lived there till around 1069 and died there in 1072 upon his return from a three year pilgrimage to the Holy Land - even though he probably didn't make it into the Holy City itself due to political changes:

1056-1074: *The Muslim rulers of Jerusalem forbid Christian pilgrims to enter the city and a massacre of unarmed Christian Pilgrims takes place there in 1064 followed by an appeal by the Byzantine Emperor to the Pope for help in 1074.*

1095: *In November Pope Urban II calls for a Crusade at the Council of Clermont in the same year that the Byzantine Empire in Eastern Europe calls on the rest of Europe for military aid against the Turks.*

1099: *The 1st Crusade reaches Jerusalem in the summer of 1099.*
1099: *15th July, Godfrey of Bouillon, Duke of Lower Loraine, forms the Knights Of St John when Jerusalem is taken, they lay down their swords, take monastic vows, and attend to injured knights, taking over the existing hospital in Jerusalem first established by the merchants of Amalfi in the Tenth Century.*

1100: *The Latin Kingdom of Jerusalem is organized as a feudal state with the Al-Aqsa mosque becoming the Royal Palace of the Kingdom of Jerusalem in 1104.*

The Reign Of King Henry I (1100-1135)

1113-1118: *The 'Independent Order of the Hospital of St John in Jerusalem' (Knights Hospitaller) is confirmed by Pope Paschal II & runs under Augustinian Monastic rule to care for all injured Crusader knights in conflicts across the Medieval world. In 1114 the Bishop of Chartres? refers in his records to a forming military order called the 'Militia Of Christ' who, it is thought, emerge in 1118 as 'The Poor Knights of the Temple of Solomon' (Knights Templar) formed by Hugh de Payens & Godfrey de St Omer essentially to protect pilgrims on the road from Jaffa to Jerusalem. It is of little doubt that they had other agendas to pursue as the order became very wealthy and famous in a relatively short period of time.*

1120: The back-story to Robyn Hoode really begins when King Henry I's only legitimate son and heir, William Adelin, dies on the 25 November 1120 in the sinking of the *'Blanche-Nef'* (White Ship) in the English Channel creating a struggle for succession that results in the conflict between King Stephen and Queen Matilda. Almost 300 lives perished in the sinking and only two survived to tell the tale. Contemporary historian William of Malmesbury also records the death of *"Richard d'Avranches, second Earl of Chester, and his brother Otheur (Arthur),... No ship ever brought so much misery to England."* It is with the Earls of Chester that our story of Robyn Hoode begins.

The importance and position of Chester in the affairs of Medieval England has been severely under-played. The Palatine Counties (or 'self-governing') of Cheshire and Lancashire, and the Baronial holdings of northern lands, held its own court at Chester equal in powers to any held in London – indeed it is possible that Chester was considered as a suitable capital for the realm at various stages in the development of the country, especially during the Roman and early medieval eras. The Saxons chose Winchester as their capital and London did not rise to prominence until the arrival of the Vikings.

1122: *Eleanor Of Aquitaine is born.*

1123-1128: *In 1123 the Knights Hospitaller pick up their swords again and follow the Templars in becoming a fully military order. In 1124 Hugh de Payens becomes the first Grand Master of the Templars and visits Europe and the UK in 1127 to rally support, which he crucially obtains from St Bernard Abbot of Clairvaux. The order is now fully Monastic and initially Augustinian before later changing to Cistercian rule.*

At this time Hugh comes to the city of Chester & meets the Earl's Of Chester and the Barons Of Halton who found the Augustinian Norton Priory in Cheshire in this year, the only Augustinian foundation in Britain to eventually attain 'Abbey' status. It is this visit that cements the allegiance of the Northern Barons primarily to the Knights Templar, a situation still existing throughout the days of Robyn Hoode.

Meanwhile, back in Jerusalem the Templars are still recorded as being only 9 knights & a few recruits in 1128. It is from this time that

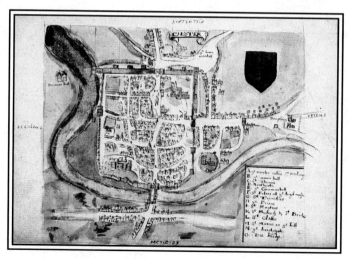

Medieval Chester As Robyn Would Have Known It.

the famous seal showing 'two knights on one horse' originates as it is thought they were so poor that they only had about four horses between them and had to ride two on a horse!

1130: *St Bernard completes "In Praise Of Knighthood" a work which combines the ideals of knighthood and monasticism forming the basis of the noble knightly society into which Robyn Hoode is later born. This is the 'code of courtesy' almost always broken by Robyn's victims in the tales giving him a clear excuse to take their money and possessions. St Bernard is also a great supporter of the female aspects of God and an ardent follower of Mary (Mother Of God) as is Robyn and all subsequent members of the order of Knights Templar.*

1129 or 1130 (Winter): The birth of Robyn Hoode takes place in the reign of King Henry the second – although the exact location for this is unknown it is most probably the medieval village of Loxley in Staffordshire on the lands of the Earls Of Chester.

In the Ballad *'Robin Hood's Birth, Breeding, Valour, And Marriage'* his father is described as 'a forester' so skillful with a bow that he could shoot two north-country miles in one shot. Beyond this any specific reference or entry for him or his name remains missing from the historic record as it was his wife who was 'noble' and he was her second husband for only a short time before passing away. However, what we can say is that living in the world of foresters obviously had a profound effect on the young Robyn Hoode and gave him an hereditary right to start his career at the same social level as his father.

His mother is stated to have been a niece of the celebrated

(indeed 'legendary') Guy, Earl of Warwick, and her brother's nick-name is 'Gamwell', a noble house-keeper and famous squire who lived at 'Great Gamwell Hall' (probably in the area around Leek in Staffordshire). Robyn's mother can be traced from the tales, and a fairly accurate family tree appears later in this book clearly identifying both her and her brother. Many years of work by gifted researchers has built a huge picture of medieval noble families accessible on the internet and indescribably helpful as leads to be checked against original documentary sources speeding this entire genealogical process up.

Robyn's birth name is sometimes recorded as 'Robert Fitzooth' (according to *'The Life & Ballads Of Robin Hood' / John Major*) but this is certainly a later invention, and he is frequently styled *"Earl Of Huntingdon"* however this could be a 'pun' on "Hunting Town" i.e. "Hunting-ton" meaning 'the forest'. It is worth remembering that the actual meanings of place-names are usually more important than the names themselves.

There is no early evidence to support either of these details, although some important characters associated with Robyn do have firm associations with the title "Earl Of Huntington" such as John The Scot, an Earl of Chester with whom Robyn grew up, and the Gisburne family who were later opponents of Robyn, but not Robyn himself. This may simply be the first incidence of associated material becoming confused over time and then being written into legend in a form not originally intended.

It is worthy of note that some other later authorities claim that Robyn was born in Locksley, Yorkshire (*'Sloan Manuscript'* 1600) at a house called *'Little Haggar's Croft'* Loxley Chase (*John Harrison, antiquarian* 1637) in the area called Hallamshire (*Roger Dodsworth, antiquarian* 17th Century).

Recently it has been discovered that there was even a tiny village clustered on the south bank of the medieval bridge over the River Dee at Chester referred to in early manuscripts as 'Loxley' which raises another new possibility.

However these sit against the earlier tradition contained in Harwood's notes upon Erdeswick's *'Survey Of Staffordshire And Its Antiquities'*, referring to Loxley near Bagot's Park, Staffordshire where he says explicitly:

"Loxley was the birth-place of Robin Hood; a rambling life led him to Tutbury, not far from his birth-place, where he married a shepherdess under the poetical name of Clorinda, having been charmed by her dexterous manner of killing a buck in the forest."

This fits extremely well with the surrounding geography and long established place name evidence found at this location, and includes the old name 'Clorinda' which may be an affectionate name for Matilda / Marian taken from an early Medieval popular figure of legend found in the May festivities. At nearby Abbots Bromley survives the famous 'Horn Dance' which rather tellingly includes 'Maid Marian' but NOT Robyn Hoode – only 'an archer' to represent a forester amongst the horned stags. This land at Bagot's Park was once owned by the 'Marmion' family in the days of Robyn Hoode. The linguistic connection to the early 'Marrion' here is obvious. The horns have also been carbon dated back to the early 11th century making them already a hundred years old at the time of Robyn Hoode and who may have witnessed, or even taken part in, this now ancient tradition.

The de Marmion family can be found to own lands almost always adjacent to areas associated with Robyn Hoode and there is no reason to doubt that Marrion would have another name or

nick-name like 'Clorinda' under which she could pursue her less lady-like occupation of female forester as she appears in the legends. Hereditary King's Champion Sir Robert Marmion of Tamworth and Scrivelsby (died in 1218) is thought to be of the same family connected to 'Maid Marian' as they owned Bagot's Park, Abbot's Bromley and Needwood Forest by Chartley. He was a Crusader and possibly also a Templar.

Slightly later in time and further north-east in Nottinghamshire, Sir John Biron is recorded in contemporary records as a *'Templar under Edward I'* and his family rose to become *'Masters Of Sherwood Forest'* showing Templar control existed in this forest region also.

The Abbot's Bromley Horn Dancers.

The early *'Foresters Manuscript'* records that:

"Randolph kept Robin fifteen winters
Dery dery downe
Till he was fifteen years old."

1130-1145: The implication is that Robyn was born in winter and somehow supported or was even accommodated as a child and young man by Ranulf II (de Gernons) Earl Of Chester (1129-1153), his family or his household.

Therefore Robyn was most probably the child of a nobleman-forester born in one of the two winters 1129/30 or 1130/31 in a village called 'Loxley' on an estate owned or managed by one of the Earl's Of Chester or his immediate family. There is no evidence of 'Saxon blood' flowing in his veins as this addition to the story is entirely a false Victorian invention.

This means that Hugh Kevelioc (Earl of Chester 1153-1181) and his son, Ranulf III de Blunderville (Earl of Chester 1181-1232), both coincide with the life of Robyn Hoode and neatly explains the 'Ranulf' connection made in William Langland's 'Piers Plowman' written around 1362 when the character 'Sloth' is made to say: *"I do not know my paternoster* (prayers) *perfectly as the priest sings it, But I know rhymes of Robin Hood and Ranulf, Earl of Chester."* Ranulf III was the last Earl of Chester to use the name 'Ranulf' so the combined *"rhymes of Robin Hood and Ranulf"* must owe their origin to between the years 1129 and 1232. As the oldest datable source currently known the importance of this reference can not be over-stressed.

Interestingly Ranulf III de Blunderville was followed by his son-in-law John the Scot (Earl of Chester 1219-1237), who was the real 'Earl of Huntingdon'. Possibly later writers assumed that Robyn had somehow inherited this title from this existing family connection but this has never been shown to be the case histori-cally? If Robyn did have a desire to use this title it may help to explain the animosity between himself and the Gisburne family.

John the Scot's grand daughter Margaret married John de Lacy, another family name highly prominent in locations directly associated with Robyn Hoode. If the later warrior Robyn had a military commander representing the Earl's of Chester there is enough evidence to suggest that it was probably a member of the de Lacy family – possibly Roger 'Hell' de Lacy.

Some authorities feel that these medieval families with direct ties to Robyn Hoode form the original source of the legends which were taken up by the family bards, minstrels, and performers, and carried round the country as these families 'progressed' around their estates and attended the various obligatory gatherings of knights and nobles. Certainly this appears to be the case with the Earls Of Chester.

1133: *The future King Henry is born on the 5ᵗʰ March 1133 at Le Mans.*

1135-1153: *Following the loss of the White Ship this period becomes known as 'The Anarchy' during which time there was a nationwide break down in law and order following a power struggle between Henry I's nominated successor, his daughter (Queen) Matilda, and the challenger, his nephew (King) Stephen of Blois. After many conflicts with Barons building castles and amassing private armies, this period ended with Matilda's son, Henry II 'Fitzempress' signing the 'Treaty Of Winchester' with Stephen in 1153 establishing himself as legitimate successor to them both. Stephen then died the following year under dubious circumstances!*

1138: *The 'Battle Of The Standard' takes place on the 22 August 1138 on Crowton Moor near Northallerton in Yorkshire. Scottish forces under King David I of Scotland face the English commanded by William le Gros (Aumale). David I of Scotland loses the battle, which is fought around a cart carrying various religious standards (hence the name), then withdraws to Carlisle.*

Although Robyn is only around eight years old when this battle takes place, it is possible that he would have been affected by the instability it represents and he may have had direct connections to the Aumale family which we will examine in the section about his family tree, some of his immediate family members may have taken part in this conflict.

The Reign Of King Stephen (1135-1154)

1139: *The Templars are finally confirmed (recognized and fully constituted) by Pope Innocent II.*

1140-1150: In the ballad *'Robin Hood And The Stranger'* we are given more information about Robin when he first meets 'Will Scarlett'.

Robin has a sister whose only son at this point is *"young Gamwell"* (William Scathelock), born and bred in 'Maxfield' (Macclesfield) and on the run for killing his father's steward, his father being the 'Earl Of Maxfield' from whom he was separated some time ago, possibly as a child.

Although the whole issue of the 'Gamwell' material is a thorny one (surviving examples of its usage being very late in terms of manuscripts), it may contain an element of earlier truth when broken down in more detail.

It basically means that Robyn's sister was married to the Earl of Macclesfield and produced a son called 'Gamwell'.

More importantly it also means that the sister's father is also Robyn's father.

This enables us to build a short family tree, especially as the "Earl's of Macclesfield" in the twelfth and thirteenth centuries were essentially the Earl's of Chester as the later separate title for Macclesfield did not yet exist. However, the important administrative and Royal town of Macclesfield and its surrounding 130 acre royal hunting forests certainly did! While the title has been imported into the story in later ages, the basic fabric of the story appears to be much earlier and consistent with known historic facts.

Given the evidence, is there a candidate for the place where Robyn Hoode spent his youth while adopted by the Earl Of Chester? Actually there is.

There is a very real possibility that the accommodation in which Robyn was housed during his 15 or 16 years serving the Earls Of Chester would have been the little known Chartley Castle, which sits next to Loxley, Bagot's Park, Doveridge, and Tutbury, in Staffordshire, and is the administrative and military centre for this area.

This amazing 'lost' ruin of a full size medieval castle, constructed by the Earls Of Chester, is virtually unknown today yet it sits next to a possible Roman enclosure, an Anglo Saxon / Norman moated site with a large bailey, and a moated Tudor manor house with fish ponds upon whose private estate it now sits. It is the Norman moated manor house to the rear of the site that would have accommodated young Robyn as the construction of the castle only began during Robyn's adult years.

Chartley Castle In Staffordshire.

1145: Robyn Hoode (age 15) is said to have been wild and extravagant resulting in bad debts for which he becomes an

outlaw and lives in the woods. However, this is an over simplistic view given the more developed tales which follow.

In the earliest tales of Robyn Hoode these woods are said to include: Barnesdale (Yorkshire), Sherwood (Nottinghamshire), and Plumpton Park / Ingleton (Cumberland).

Early sources always style Robyn simply as a 'Yeoman' which, at this point in history, means any appointed servant of a person of title. Sources from the period frequently confuse the title 'Yeoman' with many different appointments and trades as it had not yet been established as a separate title in its own right. It signifies merely 'an appointment' and does not prevent Robyn from having another practical function such as 'Noble' (with or without title), 'Knight', 'Forester', 'Archer', or even 'Outlaw' acting under the instruction of someone in a higher position of authority such as a Baron, Earl, or King. The title is also flexible as the person can 'climb' the medieval social ladder and yet still remain a 'Yeoman', or 'Youngerman' as the title first appears in the 12th century.

Like all good 'Knights' Robyn Hoode is, however, devoted to the Virgin Mary, 'Mary Mother Of God'. He does not *"rob the rich to give to the poor"* in the early ballads, he engages in 'shaming contests' that show characters for what they really are as compared to the expected codes of righteous conduct current at this time. He is more concerned with upholding audacity, charity, and courtesy, all virtues found in the codes of Medieval Knights.

In the tale *'Robin Hood And The Foresters'*, which appears in the *'Foresters Manuscript'* and later versions as the somewhat altered *'Robin Hood's Progress To Nottingham'*, the young Robyn leaves 'Randolph' and goes to a Royal archery contest at Nottingham where he is mocked by fifteen foresters who he fairly beats at shooting and drinking.

The foresters threaten to *"buffet"* him (which probably equates to a 'mob beating') so he shoots fourteen of them and kills the last as he makes his escape. The town of Nottingham is then raised against Robyn who returns to 'Loxley' and Randolph where they celebrate by getting drunk.

At this point the Sheriff of Nottingham is William Pevril 'The Younger' who is later accused of poisoning Ranulf II de Gernons (Earl Of Chester 1129-1153), undoubtedly the 'Randolph' of this story and childhood friend of Robyn Hoode.

There is little doubt of the hatred between the two noble families of Pevril and Gernons, and this act by Robyn is probably the main reason why Robyn is first outlawed in the forests which stretch all along the Great North Road (the Roman road which follows the A1(M)). The drinking celebration at the end of the story probably took place in the safety of the Norman moated manor house at Chartley back in Staffordshire.

In the ballad *'A True Tale Of Robin Hood'* written by Martin Parker in the early 17th century and published in 1632, it is recorded that: *"This Robin Hood did vindicate, His former wrongs received, For 'twas this covetous prelate, That him of land bereaved."* referring to the Abbot of St Mary's in York.

Robyn's response is to rob the Abbot's large and extensive baggage train, tie up the Abbot, take a huge sum of money, get him to bless the outlaws, then send him home reversed on his horse, an action which the Abbot reports to the king who is understandably upset.

What is important is that Robyn's lands had already been seized by St Mary's at York at this point in Robyn's youth, which Parker makes clear is the root source of his hatred of such clergy and a big contributing factor in him becoming an outlaw.

In the *'Garland'* tale *'Robin Hood's Birth, Breeding, Valour, And Marriage'* the character Gamwell (William de Roumare (2) in the father's side family tree) says to Robyn: *"Cousin Robyn, thou'st go no more home, But tarry here, and dwell with me, Thou shalt have my land when I die, and till then, Thou shalt be the staff of my age."* This could identify the land ultimately seized by St Mary's at York.

The eventual 'rightful heir' would have been William de Roumare (3), who turns out upon close examination to be none other than Will Scarlet (Gamwell Junior) who is also said to have had lands seized in later tales.

1146: *The 2nd Crusade begins & the Templars adopt their distinctive 'Cross Pattee' logo in red and white with Papal approval. These colours are purely ceremonial as actual combat outfits would be shades of brown, orange, yellow, dark blue, and black to blend into desert terrain. Armour, shields and often*  *weapons would be allowed to rust and be painted or 'dulled down', coats of arms would be kept to a minimum so only friendly soldiers knew who the nobles were. Nobles were targets for being taken captive and frequently held for ransom by the opposition.*

1146-1149: In an interesting story in the *'Foresters Manuscript'* titled *'Robin Hood's Fishing'* Robyn (probably aged 15 or 16) pretends to be a fisherman named 'Symon Of The Lee' or 'Simon Over The Lea', based at Whitby or Scarborough where he promises to work for 3 years on a ship owned by a 'widow of Scarborough'. He is not very successful and wishes he was back in 'Plumpton Park' until he uses his bow to capture a 'French ship' with '1200 pounds' on board and builds a chapel

on Whitby Strand. Possibly this sets the scene for all the 'outlawry' that follows?

> *"For yon French robbers on the sea,*
> *They will not spare of us one man,*
> *But carry us to the coast of France,*
> *And lay us in the prison strong."*

'Robin Hood And The Fisherman' from 'Robin Hood's Garland' first published 1670.

At this stage Viking (pirate) raids were still taking place along the East Coast, which had seen a great deal of such conflicts down the years. 'Vikings' or 'Norsemen' (men of the north) were known to originate from the Norman lands in northern France (Normans essentially being Vikings) which is a convincing detail which rings true in this early tale.

Scarborough Castle contains evidence for Bronze Age, Iron Age, Roman, and Saxon development, with evidence on the Roman Station site for a Saxon Chapel thought to have been destroyed during the invasion of Harald Hadrada in 1066. This 'travesty' may have been the inspiration for Robyn considering building a new chapel in 1149.

Evidence for a settlement in the vicinity of Scarborough harbor dates from around 1157-1164 as part of a settlement which grew up round a wooden fortress erected by William le Gros, Count of Aumale, (grand-nephew of William The Conqueror), after he received the Earldom of York in 1138 as a reward for King Stephen's victory at the *Battle Of The Standard* in Yorkshire (where William Aumale commanded the English army). This timber castle, owned and garrisoned by the English hero-knight William 'le Gros' Aumale, would be the one to which Robyn Hoode would have traveled in 1146-1149, and there is evidence to say that the Marmion family also owned lands here in the area around Robin Hood's Bay. As noted in the later family tree, Robyn also has close ties to the 'Aumale' family through his mother.

Before 1500 Robin Hood's Bay was a more important port than Whitby and possessed Old St Stephen's Church on the hillside at Raw above the village, which replaced a 'Saxon' church there (finally demolished in 1821). This is most likely to be the chapel on 'Whitby Strand' referred to, which Robyn would have effectively re-built in stone from the original Saxon timber structure. This was common as the Normans clearly viewed the tiny timber Saxon chapels as inferior structures and embarked on an almost universal policy of up-grading them wherever they were found. The chapel at Scarborough Castle was private, already constructed, and within the castle bounds, thus ruling this out as the one built by Robyn.

Chronicler monk William of Newburgh recorded Scarborough Castle as a gate tower, curtain wall, dry moat, and chapel. King Henry II eventually repossessed the site and built the first stone castle there between 1159 and 1169, ten years after the young Robyn Hoode had left.

Bound into the same story in the *'Foresters Manuscript'* as *'Robin Hood's Fishing'* is the interesting encounter already mentioned where Robyn kills 15 corrupt foresters who are buried *"in Nottingham church yard, laid all in a row"* - an interesting discovery awaiting future archaeologists perhaps?

1150: It is said that the meeting of Robyn and Little John took place when Robyn was around 20 years of age and that John was, at this time, already seven feet tall.

In *'Robin Hood's Garland'* (first 16 tales collected and published in 1670) Little John says to the Sheriff of Nottingham in *'Robin Hood, Little John, And The Sheriff'*:

> *"I was born," he said, "in Holderness,*
> *If I may my mother believe:*
> *And when I amongst my kindred dwell,*
> *Men call me Reynold Greenleaf."*

Later traditional tales tell that the two fought with staffs to see who would cross a narrow bridge over a brook first. Robyn lost the match, which is common in early tales, and enlists Little John, but it already appears that Robyn had collected a notable 'band of merry men'. Other earlier Ballads place their first meeting as teenagers in the house of Gamwell (Senior) during the time of Robyn's adoption where John is appointed as Robyn's 'page'.

John is always given as younger than Robyn so both stories may be true with Robyn first meeting John as a young page, losing contact with him during the years in Whitby and Scarborough, to be reunited with an older and much stronger John many years later who is then 'initiated' into Robyn's service following a 'trial by combat'.

In the original story this may have been done with swords not staffs but was probably felt to be too violent and, therefore, diluted to 'staffs' in later tales. Little John also has a 'nick-name' like Marian's 'Clorinda', he goes under the pseudonym

of 'Reynold Greenleaf'.

Local squire William Shuttleworth had the grave of Little John in Hathersage Church, Derbyshire, opened in the late 1700s and the thigh bone from the skeleton they found was measured at 29.5 inches by the woodsman Mr. Hinchcliffe. William still had the thigh bone in 1784 but it was taken by one Sir George Strickland on a visit and never seen again. The upper half of a medieval grave slab with the later  inscribed initials 'L.J.' still resides inside the church porch and represents the recognisable cross of a Templar / Forester Knight, formerly having two shields above it which are now sadly blank, and a worn outside border lacking any inscription. However, this gives us a clear and authentic indication of the type of iconography we should be searching for when looking at later 13th century burials associated with Robyn and his men.

In *'Robin Hood And The Tanner'* the main character Arthur-a-Bland says to Robyn *"But tell me, O tell me, where is Little John? Of him I fain would hear; For we are allied by the mother's side, And he is my kinsman dear."*

When John arrives he recognizes Arthur the Tanner by name and they are very glad to meet, the obvious implication being that they are long separated half-brothers having the same mother but different fathers as was common amongst medieval noble families where the woman has re-married. In Medieval times noble women who were inheritors of property, land and wealth were virtually compelled to re-marry unless they took religious vows or bought their freedom.

Moving on to other well known members of Robyn's gathering band of outlaws - the main story concerning William Scathelock is in two distinct and separate parts entitled *'Robin Hood And The Stranger: Pt.1. Robin Hood And Will Scarlet, Pt.2. The Encounter With The Giants'* and appears in early *'Garland's*. For no good reason it appears to have thwarted all attempts at sensible interpretation, usually being dismissed as 'nothing more than a legend' mainly on the basis of the use of the word 'giant'!

English Oak In The Macclesfield Forest.

In part one of this story Robyn Hoode goes out into the forest and meets a smart young nobleman in a silk doublet and red stockings (hose). They prove to be virtually equal in archery and sword play so Robyn calls a halt to sword fighting and asks who he is? He replies: *"In Maxfield (Macclesfield) town I was bred and born; "My name is young Gamwell, For killing my own father's steward, I am forced to this English wood, And for to seek an uncle of mine, Some call him Robin Hood."* He later adds *"I am his own sister's son."* Robin is joined by Little John and

they decide *"Will Scathelock he shall be."* ('Scarlet' only in later versions of the story).

It is however possible that William Scathelock and Will Scarlet are in fact two brothers who have been confused by later translators changing the name 'Scathelock' (meaning 'lock-smasher') to Scarlet (meaning 'red') on the false assumption that they are the same person. We will return to this issue later. Meanwhile:

In part two Robyn meets one of four ladies riding out from London to all parts of England seeking champions to fight a *'foreign Prince'* who is threatening to take a princess off the king as his bride unless he and his two *'giants'* can be defeated. Robyn is mortified and he goes to the proposed midsummer tournament in London accompanied by Little John and Will Scathelock disguised as pilgrims from the Holy Land. They are given arms, defeat the three challengers one-on-one, and the princess chooses to marry Will Scathelock, who is then identified at the event by his father, the Earl of Maxfield, as his long lost son.

Tackling the thorny issues contained in this story head on:

We do not know in what year this story is set, although the details may indicate we are still firmly in the period of internal civil war between Stephen and Matilda known as 'The Anarchy', between 1135 and 1153. Mention of *'Aragon'* in the story dates it after 1137, and the inclusion of Little John probably takes it to after 1150, narrowing the field to the four summers of 1150, 1151, 1152, or 1153.

We are not told which *'king'* the *'princess'* is daughter of, or if she is 'legitimate' or 'illegitimate'. While Welsh and Irish kings are highly unlikely to be in London, the opposite can be said of English and Scottish Kings. We can rule out King Stephen (1135-1154) as two of his three daughters are dead by this time, and the other is known to be the Countess of Boulogne.

However, 'Scotland Yard' got its name from a permanent 12th century palace standing on the site used by the Kings of Scotland who were required to come to London every year to acknowledge their subordination to the monarch of England as shown by royal commands surviving from 970 and 1170. Between 1135 and 1153 this would have been the 'House of Dunkeld' in the form of a frequent visitor to London, King David I of Scotland, Earl of Northumbria (and then holder of Huntingdon). As already noted, in 1138 David's army fought at the Battle Of The Standard and were defeated by the English army led by William, Earl of Aumale, the family directly associated with Robyn Hoode and now also Will Scarlet.

While he only had one male heir (Henry, Earl of Northumberland, who died from an unknown illness) by Matilda, Countess of Huntingdon, she had three daughters, Matilda of St Liz (who married Robert Fitz Richard, then married Saer De Quincy), Claricia, and Hodierna, both of whom are thought to have died young and unmarried. Either of these could easily be the *'princess'* betrothed to Will Scarlett, a lady who obviously does not survive long enough to appear in later stories.

So what enemy would be so bad that it would cause Robyn, John, and Will to defend a Scottish princess?

The *'giants'* at the tournament are described as: "...*the proud prince of Arragon,*" (the kingdom in Northern Spain founded in 1137 under Queen Petronilla) who says "*I swear by the Alcoran.*" Robyn describes him as "*Thou tyrant Turk, thou infidel,*" and they are "*With serpents hissing on their helms, Instead of feathered plumes.*" These three *'giants'* are what we would identify today as two Viking mercenaries led by a Moorish knight from the newly founded Spanish kingdom trying to exert greater authority through a royal marriage. Far from being fantasy, this is perfectly accurate for the period in which this story is set. For example, in 1151 King Eystein II of Norway sailed through Orkney threatening King David I and asserting continued Viking control over parts of Scotland, just one of many such conflicts that continued to affect the whole of Britain and Europe.

So it is that a story dismissed as 'complete fantasy' by scholars of past ages does, actually, stand detailed examination using known historic facts.

1150-1160: Possibly the most famous and repeated story of Robyn Hoode and his complete outlaw band begins in the forests of 'Bernysdale' accompanied by Little John where they capture a 'poor knight' (later 'Richard at the Lee') who has lost his son after his son slew a 'knight of Lancashire' and the knight has gone into debt to the Abbot of St Mary's Abbey in York trying to raise funds for his son's release. It also appears from his scruffy red and white livery that he is a Templar. The outlaws steal the Abbot's money from traveling monks and give it to the knight who then goes to York and repays the crooked Abbot gaining back his lands – meanwhile John's attention is drawn to the Sheriff of Nottingham (leading to the next tale).

The Area Of The Medieval Forest Of Barnesdale South Yorkshire.

Little John goes to the Sheriff and demonstrates his sword and archery skills and the Sheriff is inspired to hold an archery contest which includes:

Lytell Johan, Robyn Hode, Gylberte 'white hande', Scatheloke, Lytell Much, and 'good' Reynolde.

The outlaws are recognized and flee to the castle of the poor knight 'Richard at the Lee' who is then arrested. In escaping from the archery contest Little John is injured by an arrow in the knee and takes about a year to recover (1150-1151).

A verse contained in 'Robin Hood's Garland' (published 1670) gives the location of the poor knight's castle in 'The Knight And The Monks Of Saint Mary's Abbey':

"His lady met him at the gate – At home in Uterysdale."
(Wrysedale).

Robyn then takes the fight to the Sheriff and the evil Sheriff is killed on the streets of Nottingham without hesitation by an arrow from Robin (and sometimes beheaded) and the Sheriff's men defeated.

1153: Some believe that this was when Robyn Hoode was initially outlawed making the evil Sheriff a character we have already met once before, William Pevril 'The Younger' (Sheriff of Nottingham between 1129-1153), who would have been killed some time in the year 1153. This is the same William Pevril who was histori-cally accused of poisoning Ranulf II (de Gernons) Earl Of Chester (1129-1153), Robyn's adopted parent.

Peveril Castle at Castleton, Derbyshire, now became forfeit and property of the Crown for the next 50 years, as attested to by several surviving historical documents and charters surviving

Peveril Castle Ruins Castleton Derbyshire.

from this time.

In one version of a very late 18th century Robyn Hoode tale *'Queen Catherine'*, King Henry announces to Sir Richard Lee: *"Well it is knowen ffrom thy pedigree, Thou came from Gawiins blood."* This being 'Sir Gawain' of the Arthur legends and Richard's ancestry is therefore apparently North Welsh, Cheshire or Derbyshire borders (if this is a genuine survival from earlier legends).

1153-1157: In the early tales contained in *'Robin Hood's Garland'* (published in 1670), with permission from Robyn Hoode, Little John agrees to work in the employ of the Sheriff of Nottingham in *'Robin Hood, Little John, And The Sheriff'* for a year after an (unspecified) archery contest.

This story is interesting as it is evidently not based on the similar more famous one just previously quoted and contained in the *'Geste'*. An early 15th century dramatic fragment exists of *'Robyn*

Hod and the Shryff off Notyngham' in Cambridge, Trinity College, which contains a few brief verses from which this sufficiently different story can be reconstructed.

An un-named Knight volunteers to capture Robyn for the Sheriff and they meet, challenging each other to first an archery contest, which Robyn wins, then stone throwing, tossing a wooden pole (axle), throwing stones, wrestling (in which the knight throws Robyn), then Robyn blows his horn for help, they fight with swords with Robyn the winner, and he cuts off the knight's head. Robin then dresses in the knight's clothing and sticks the severed head in his hood.

We then move to a conversation between two outlaws:

The outlaws point out that Robyn and his men have been captured by the Sheriff and they intend to rescue them with the aid of 'Frere Tuke' who is a good bowman (this represents the earliest surviving reference to Friar Tuck). They arrive at the prison gates and challenge the Sheriff who brings out Robyn (who he has evidently captured) and the others, the Sheriff assuming he now has them all at his mercy . . .

> *"Come thou forth, thou fals outlawe.*
> *Thou shall be hagyde and y-drawe."*

Here the surviving story fragment ends – but we can assume from other surviving sources that the combined forces of Robyn Hoode and Friar Tuck overcome the Sheriff, escape, and live to fight another day.

What is equally intriguing is that no Sheriff has yet been identified for Nottingham between the years 1153 and 1157 which would fit the scenario that Robyn and his men spend four years infiltrating and interfering with this appointment, possibly repeating the killing of another 'unsuitable' Sheriff, or inexperienced stand-in Sheriff, who attempts their capture. It also proves the inclusion of 'Frere Tuke' at a very early date.

The violence shown in this story is thought to help prove this very early date but is by no means unique. In a 15th Century version of the *'Geste'* Robyn robs a party of monks in *'Robin Hood And The Monk'*, killing a monk and his servant, and in *'Robin Hood And Guy Of Gisborne'* Robyn takes Sir Guy's head by the hair and sticks it on the end of his bow, slashing the face with an *'Irish knife'* so that it's virtually unrecognizable and taking it home for all to see! In some later tales Robyn pretends to be Guy and that the disfigured head is that of Robyn.

The early tales of Robyn and his men are simply more aggressive. Robyn shoots the Sheriff with an arrow and/or beheads him for his treachery, and kills monks. John also kills a monk, and Much the Miller's son beheads the monk's little page to silence him. Even the poor knight 'Richard at the Lee's son is in trouble for killing a knight and his page while jousting.

The first person on written record as asserting that Robyn was *'a good man'* was actually a sheriff's clerk writing a comment on a parliamentary return as late as the year 1432, 300 years after the birth of Robyn Hoode!

Early Morning View Over Sherwood Forest Nottinghamshire.

So Who Is This Robyn Hoode And His Band Of Outlaws?

What we are dealing with in the 12th century is a frustratingly complicated and fluid social structure, even amongst the nobility, that often defies specific definition and through which characters move at different times in their lives.

At the top stands the king – but even this simple statement is complicated by various inter-family conflicts, inheritance rows, illegitimate claims, and even powerful noble families with large private armies and eyes on the throne (such as those in the north).

Not everyone actually knew who the ruling monarch was until word spread. Hence we have the later tensions between Richard and John, with John often claiming kingship while Richard was still alive, and the Earls and Barons such as those at Chester, Lancaster, and York, who are known to have ruled the north almost as 'lesser kings' during Richard's absence. The power of the Earls and Barons depended on the size of their land holdings, private armies, number of fortifications, relationship to the king, religious and knightly vows, and how many of them were willing to band together to form a significant force.

Added to this we have a small number of incredibly powerful ecclesiastics, Abbots with the full backing of church and state, no threat to the specific role of 'king' but wielding as great, if not frequently more, power over the population, and with the full force and riches of the church and pope behind them. Robyn Hoode had a particular dislike of this category that are portrayed as greedy, unjust, and not fulfilling their religious office.

Once outside this upper group, things continue to remain complicated. The originally Viking tradition of legitimate and illegitimate sons wanting to enter this upper group by taking property and position continues - hence we have the young men occupying disputed territories and taking military appointments of all kinds from those above them. There even existed the tradition of those in the upper group paying 'scutage' or 'shield money' for those in this lower group to take military assignments on their behalf. The king would order a sum to be paid from each 'knight's fee', such as one mark or one pound, to provide wages for soldiers and mercenaries, so that he didn't have to expose his own people to the risks of war. It is likely that Robyn Hoode, Little John, and possibly the 'Scarlet's', originally fall into this category of 'appointed mercenaries' acting on behalf of the northern Earls and Barons then ultimately under the King.

Below this category sits the developing group of 'appointed professionals' which include the developing yeomen ('youngermen' or appointed servants), foresters, minstrels and performers, tradesmen and those who are part of a 'guild', physicians, philosophers, those in monastic life such as monks, nuns and friars, and anyone essentially holding 'rights' prior to Magna Carta.

At the bottom of the tree sit the peasants and workers who generally lived at a reasonable standard in Medieval Europe unless misfortune, sickness or disability rendered them beggars. It appears that none of Robyn's followers fall into this category.

While society was male dominated, it was not out of the question for women to follow basically the same social structure as men in all respects from the Queen down, often wielding equal or greater power than her male counterpart. In the tales of Robyn Hoode we see several strong female characters equally as good as men such as Marian Clorinda (Forester / Huntress), Dervorguilla Of Gallway (Daughter of David of Scotland and Matilda of Chester, inheritor of Cumberland and Galloway), Queen Matilda (who makes a try for the throne against Stephen), and Eleanor Of Aquitaine (the Queen who rules her family with an 'iron fist' and produces King Richard and King John).

Looking more specifically at some important characters that appear in records in this time period:

Ranulf II (de Gernons) Earl Of Chester (1129-1153) was a

hugely important (and frequently overlooked) figure in Medieval history being instrumental in securing Henry II and the Plantagenets to the English throne for which he was granted many Staffordshire lordships. It is a well documented historical fact that among these lordships were all the estates of *'Radulphus filius odonis'*, the Latinized form of 'Od', 'Odo', or 'Hod'. These estates lay dispersed about Staffordshire with others in Shropshire, Warwickshire, and other counties, and one of the 'Odo' daughters inherited the Lordship of another 'Lockesley' down in Warwickshire. As noted, the 'Earl Ranulph' of Robyn's life-time is the grandson of the Ranulph who died in 1153.

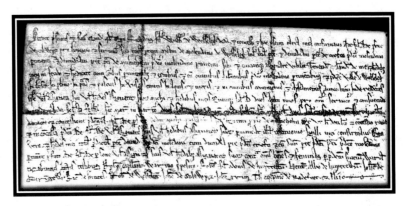

The 'real' Robyn Hoode may well be the 'Robert Fil Odonis' ('Odo' or 'Hode') who witnessed the sale of the Mill at Wolseley (within 3 miles of Loxley, Staffordshire,) in the early part of the reign of Henry III (1216-1272). In this same geographic area 'William Hod' faced a charge of robbery in 1258 (*'Salt Society's Staffordshire Collections Vol 4 p136'*), and a different 'William Hod' conveyed a stolen deer to the house of the previous senior 'Mr Hod' (who was then dead) 13 years later in 1271. This younger 'William Hod' lived *"... near Penkridge, upon the confines of the forest."* If nothing else this establishes this family and name in the area concerned.

Now returning to the time-line:

The Reign Of King Henry II (1154-1189)

Robyn hod inscherewod stod, hodud and hathud and hosut and schod
Four and thuynti arowus he bar in hits hondus.

Robin Hood in Sherwood stood, hooded and hated and hosed and shod
Four and twenty arrows he bore in his hands.

Scribbled verse in a Lincoln Cathedral Manuscript C1410.

1154 – 1189: *King Henry II Plantagenet (Henry Of Anjou) takes the throne starting the Plantagenet dynasty. He marries the rich, beautiful, and powerful former wife of King Louis VII of France, Eleanor Of Aquitaine, who divorces Louis and marries Henry 'for love' just 6 weeks later in Westminster Abbey and already 5 months pregnant. She has been to the Holy Land with her former husband on the Second Crusade and even led a special 'ladies crusade'. She eventually gives*

Henry 8 sons including Richard and John, but continues to wield power behind the scenes during both of their future reigns.

1154 - 1157: Around the years 1154-1157 a pardon from the new King Henry II Plantagenet follows for Robyn and his men killing the corrupt Sheriff (or Sheriffs) of Nottingham.

The King here in most later stories of Robyn's life is almost always wrongly given as an unspecified *'Edward'* (first, second, or third, no one knows?) who probably appealed to the views of the listeners when this story was developed yet again for a new audience, or was simply a 'safe guess' for various authors over the years.

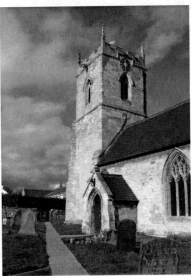

During this period of Robyn's 'forgiveness' Robyn also builds a chapel in 'Barnysdale' dedicated to Mary Magdalene. This would date this chapel foundation (again in stone) to around 1154-1160.

The only Medieval chapel left standing in the whole of the old medieval Barnsdale area is St Peter's Church at Kirk Smeaton which is recorded as already established in Saxon form in the Domesday Survey of 1086, and has surviving stonework dateable to the 12th and 13th Centuries appropriate to the Robyn Hoode period. One solitary Medieval Knight's tomb lid, built into the rear outside wall of the bell tower, shows that Knights who followed the Virgin Mary were burying their dead here in Robyn's time. It also appears to be of a type familiar in this area as Forester / Templar.

1154-1160: Robyn Hoode collects his band of outlaws which are now said to include:

Little John (or John Little, Lyttel, in later stories given the surname 'Nailor') / William Scathelock (Scadlock or Scarlett, thought to mean 'lock-smasher') / George a-Green (pinder or 'pound-keeper' – an enclosure for animals) of Wakefield / Much, a miller's son / Friar (or Father) Tuck / Marrion (Marian, Matilda or Clorinda) - 'maid' and sometimes of noble birth), Will Scarlett (is said to be the brother of William Scathelock in stories after C1660) / David of Doncaster / plus '70-110 or more Archers'.

Inevitably there are some tales of Robyn Hoode and his band of outlaws that stubbornly defy all attempts to place them in time or to authenticate them in any way.

Some examples include: *'Robyn Hoode Rescuing Will Stutley'* which involves the rescue of the arrested Will by Little John from the hands of the Sheriff who intends to hang him, and has a very similar plot to *'Robin Hood Rescues The Widow's Three Sons From The Sheriff'*, *'Robin Hood Saves Three Deer-Stealers From Being Hanged'* and *'Robin Hood Rescuing The Three Squires'*. All that can confidently be said is that Robyn and John saved various woodsmen condemned to hang during their careers as outlaws!

One plot variation in *'Robin Hood Rescues The Widow's Three Sons From The Sheriff'* is that it ends with the death of the Sheriff; *"They took the gallows from the slack, They set it in the glen; They hanged the proud sheriff on that, And released their own three men."* The question which may never be answered here is: "Were any of the 21 known Sheriff's of Nottingham during the outlaw reign of Robyn Hoode (in the 70 years between say 1150-1220) ever hanged?" There are at least two other sheriffs who die at the hand of Robyn, neither of them by hanging, who we will come to later. Did this hanging incident occur in the four years when the names of Sheriffs are missing – between 1153 and 1157?

In 'Robin Hood And The Potter', 'Robin Hood And The Beggar', 'Robin Hood And The Tanner', 'Robin Hood And Curtall Friar', 'Robin Hood And The Shepherd', 'Robin Hood's Delight' 'Robin Hood And The Tinker', 'Robin Hood And The Ranger', and 'Robin Hood And Little John', Robyn picks a fight or challenge with a stout character who proves to be as good as, or better than, himself and either asks them to join his outlaw band, shows some fault in their honesty and chivalry, or swaps places with them so he can enter Nottingham and accomplish some task. This appears to be a standard pattern for Robyn's activities and a well used plot-line. In almost every case Robyn issues the new recruit with his 'livery' or heraldic badge of office, which further supports the case for him being of noble birth and position.

The only interesting plot addition to these 'challenge tales' is that 'Robin Hood And The Curtall Friar' takes the story to Fountain's Abbey where the archer-monk turns out to have been keeper of the Abbey dogs for the last seven years and, in the late adaptation of the encounter with Richard The Lionheart 'King Richard And Robin Hood', the king disguises himself and his party as monks and rides out from Fountains Abbey. These additions to the story seem to have occurred in the 17th century when relics of Robyn were being shown at a well on the Abbey site.

Robin Hood's Well At Fountains Abbey – Final Location For Robin's Relics.

In 'Robin Hood's Golden Prize' we have the rare identification of his two opponents being 'Benedicite' (Benedictines), two horse back priests wearing black, who prove to be dishonest. Fitting a similar plot line, in 'Robin Hood's Delight' Little John and Will Scarlet join Robyn in a one-on-one fight with three of King Henry's deer-keepers who have strayed into Robyn's territory and they end up 'drinking themselves friends' in Nottingham. Although a great deal is made of the mention of 'King Edward' as the monarch in versions of 'The Geste', in this early tale the three foresters clearly state: "We three," replied the keeper, 'belong to King Henry (1154-1189), and are keepers of his deer." clearly placing it somewhere in these early years.

In 'Robin Hood And The Ranger' Robyn states: "These thirteen long summers, I'm sure, My arrows I here have let fly," which gives us a possible date for this tale of around 1163.

In 'Robin Hood And The Tinker' the Tinker of Banbury has a "... warrant from the king" for the capture of Robyn Hoode which probably places this story even later during the reign of King John (1199-1216), but it is impossible to be certain.

The famous adaptations of the 'Gest' story 'Robin Hood, Little John, And The Sheriff', 'The Shooting Match At Nottingham', and 'Robin Hood And The Golden Arrow' all involve the Sheriff holding an archery contest in order to identify and capture Robyn Hoode and follow the story plot already outlined and dated to somewhere between 1150 and 1153 with the death of Sheriff William Pevril 'The Younger'.

1157: *Richard is born to Eleanor Of Aquitaine at Beaumont Palace Oxford on the 8th September 1157.*

1157: As stated, it is not known who the Sheriff of Nottingham was between 1153 and 1157, but there is some confusion in the stories which make it look like Robyn killed at least two Sheriffs in two separate and somewhat different stories ('A

Lyttell Geste Of Robyn Hode' The Archery Contest and *'Robyn Hod and the Shryff off Notyngham').*

In the *'Garland'* version of *'The Archery Contest'* Robyn finds the Sheriff and says before killing him and cutting off his head:

"*These seven years, by God's dear worth,*
I have not gone so fast on foot:"

This clearly implies that Robyn has been the opponent of the Sheriff of Nottingham from his arrival in the green-wood in 1150 until now, and that it is perhaps the year 1157 in which this particular Sheriff dies. Robyn then needs to familiarize himself with the new Sheriff and two ballads follow basically the same plot *'Robin Hood And The Butcher'* and the earlier *'Robin Hood And The Potter'*:

In the *'Garland'* version of the tale of *'Robin Sells Pots At Nottingham'* a potter is stopped on the road and switches identity with Robyn who goes to Nottingham and sells the pots for a fraction of their worth. The last few assorted pots he then gives as a free gift to the Sheriff's wife which results in him dining with the Sheriff and joining in with an archery contest between a couple of the Sheriff's men. Robyn wins and the Sheriff wishes he could meet Robyn Hoode which is swiftly arranged for the next day.

On leaving Nottingham with the Sheriff, Robyn gives the Sheriff's wife a ring as a gift and promises a horse. Only when they encounter Little John and Robyn's men in the woods does Robyn reveal his true identity, robs the Sheriff, but sends him home riding the woman's horse Robyn promised to his wife. The wife thinks the robbery good payment for a free horse and pots, the potter joins Robyn's band, chivalry is shown to have been done, but most importantly this must be a new Sheriff as

he clearly does not recognize Robyn. Robyn also has an entirely different approach towards this Sheriff and his wife.

There are two possible candidates for this Sheriff, both from the same family, and this is probably the first of them between 1157 and 1170, Sir Robert Fitz Ranulf.

1165-1184: *At some point between these dates William of Tyre writes his 'History of the Kingdom of Jerusalem' also called 'History of the Deeds Done Beyond The Sea' ('Historia rerum in partibus trans- marinis gestarum') which brings vivid tales of the Crusades back to Europe.*

1167: *King John is born at Beaumont Palace Oxford on the 24th December 1167.*

There is a strange tale in the Foresters Manuscript entitled 'Robyn Hoode And The Old Wife' (which appears to be a version of 'Robin Hood And The Bishop') in which Robyn falls asleep "Betwixt a Cragg and a stony Rock" and wakes to find the Sheriff and his men riding towards him.
   Robyn then flees to the house of an old woman he has previously helped with money for clothes and shoes and changes clothes with her. The Sheriff arrests her assuming she's Robyn and carries her off to 'King Henry' as the real Robyn escapes still wearing her clothes. The old woman finally convinces the Sheriff she's not Robyn by telling him "lift up my legg and see" and Robyn's men recognize him because he has a beard! Robyn later returns the clothes and pays her twenty pounds.

As the king is 'Henry' and the Sheriff doesn't immediately execute Robyn it is probably safe to set this story again between 1157 and 1170 during the internship of Sir Robert Fitz Ranulf.

Shady Pathway Sherwood Forest Nottinghamshire.

1169: *Saladin preaches a Holy War against the Christians.*

1170: *The famous murder of Thomas A Beckett takes place by 4 knights supposedly acting on behalf of King Henry II, who is deeply upset by their actions. As part of his penance the king invites the Carthusians, monastic 'freres' (not 'Friars'), to establish a charterhouse at Witham, Somerset, and they are followed by the Grandmontines whose first foundation of around 1204 was in Yorkshire, followed by Shropshire, then Herefordshire in 1225 under a member of the de Lacy family (Walter de Lacy), clearly establishing rapid and relevant monastic development in the days of 'Friar' Tuck.*

1173-1174: *Hugh de Kevelioc and other northern barons join the 'Baron's Revolt' against King Henry II in favour of the Scots. King William (The Lion) of Scotland invades Northumbria in 1173 and takes Alnwick as his base in 1174. Despite an extensive force including Flemish (Belgian-Dutch) mercenaries, William then splits his army into three and is defeated and captured by a force of only 400 mounted English knights under Ranulf de Glanvill at the Battle of Alnwick on* *the 13ᵗʰ July 1174. After this Hugh de Kevelioc's estates are seized by the crown for supporting the Scots, but restored in 1177. Hugh then joins Henry's campaign in Ireland.*

1173: There is an entry in the 'Royal Court Rolls' for the "County Of Cumberland" (for May 1199 and quoted in full a little further on) which states that Robyn Hoode ('Holdelme') and his father 'Udard' held Carlisle Castle under King Henry II successfully against the Scots for 3 months in 1173 when Robyn would be aged around 42-43.

1174-1177: *In 1174 William de Ferrers captures Nottingham Castle from Richard de Lucy (Warden of the Realm) who appears to have temporarily taken control of it from William FitzRanulf.*

Historically Sir Robert Fitz Ranulf (Sheriff of Nottingham 1157-1170) and William FitzRanulf (Sheriff of Nottingham 1170-1177) would be the Sheriffs with whom Robyn has many encounters in stories over the twenty years between 1157 and 1177. Evidently Robyn's activities in Nottingham up to 1157 had succeeded in eventually bringing in 'the good guy's, however this was not to last.

It is notable that Scottish writers should take an interest in Robyn's later life as the very early story 'Robin Hood And Guy Of Gisborne' appears to concern Robyn's encounter with a Scottish Knight and mercenary bounty-hunter acting on behalf of the Sheriff of Nottingham and who wears a *'capull-hide'* or 'horse skin'. (Gisburn is held by the Scottish knight William de Brus at this time - later an avid supporter of King John).

Evidently this story is set towards the end of Robyn's outlaw days as it opens with Little John captured by the Sheriff, two of Robyn's men dead, Will Scarlet on the run, and Robyn being hunted by the Mercenary who is already aware of

Robyn and Robyn of him! Robyn says *"Thou hast been a traitor all thy life, Which thing must have an end."*

Guy is beaten, Robyn cuts off his head and mutilates it with an *'Irish knife'*, then uses the head, clothes and horn to look like Guy and pretend that Guy has actually killed Robyn. The Sheriff falls for the disguise and Little John is rescued, John shooting the Sheriff in his side with an arrow as he makes his escape.

From his attitude this is evidently not the same Sheriff encountered in *'Robin Sells Pots At Nottingham'* and it is obviously later in Robyn's outlaw life. If we rule out members of the Fitz Ranulf family (who appear to have tolerated Robyn) we are left with Selo de Giendara in 1177 or Ralph Murdac between 1180 and 1190 as Sheriffs we have names for. This story probably dates from the late 1170s.

1177-1190: In 1177 Selo de Giendara is Sheriff, in 1180 Ralph Murdac, until 1190 when Roger de Lacy is the next Sheriff which ties in well with the death of Henry II Plantagenet in 1189 and the start of the reign of King Richard 'The Lionheart'.

Nottingham castle then remains for a time in the control of members of the Earl of Chester's extended family of knights in the form of Sheriffs Ranulf, Lacy, and Ferrers.

1185: *Temple Church in London is consecrated by Patriarch Heraclius of Jerusalem.*

1187: *On the 2nd October Saladin and his army re-captures Jerusalem.*

The Reign Of King Richard I (1189-1199)

"Thus still he lived by robbery,
Throughout the northern parts;"

'A True Tale Of Robin Hood' by Martin Parker, published 1632.

1189-1199: *King Richard I*  *Plantagenet (Richard The Lionheart) is notified of his father's death while he is in Normandy in July 1189, takes the throne and immediately heads to the Holy Land with Philip Of France on the Third Crusade in 1191 which ends with the re-capture of Acre in 1192. Richard is shipwrecked and captured by Duke Leopold Of Austria who sells him to Emperor Henry VI of Germany apparently then costing his brother John a huge ransom extracted from England for his release in 1194. In his entire reign King Richard spends a total of only 6 months in England and reliable historical chroniclers record the following:*

1189: King Richard's England Visit 1 (5 months):

Richard's itinerary looked something like this: Winchester 15th August, 3rd September he is in London for his coronation and stays on for the 4th and 5th where his first act as king is to grant 100 marks to the Cistercians (monks) drawn from various of his own properties.

There is a General Council at Pipewell on the 15th September. He is notified that Templars, Hospitallers and Crusaders have attacked Acre through August, September, and October, then John Of Anagni, cardinal of St Mark and official messenger, reaches Dover 20th November where they de-brief for 2 weeks.

King William Of Scotland visits Richard and pays him ten thousand marks in allegiance (thus 'buying' Scotland), then on the 14th December Richard crosses the Channel on Crusade.

Knights Of The Lion - King Richard's 'Pride Of Lions':

In the earliest surviving depictions of King Richard I and those of the Third Crusade, the king is shown to be using a single black 'lion rampant' facing to the viewers left (his right) on a plain shield with a red-orange background. (It is thought that only much later did the number of lions increase to two and possibly three and become of  'passant guardant' linear design). This detail only becomes significant when looking at the supporters of the king, especially in the north.

It appears that King Richard I created his own personal order or 'Pride of Lions' by granting permission for the use of his 'lion rampant' design, in various colour combinations, to significant rulers of the northern counties in the later 12th century. It is almost certain that this 'conclave' of powerful kings and northern nobles would ultimately have been the organization under which Robyn served and that they met frequently at various times during the year to plan politics, strategy and law.

At this time the poet Chretien de Troye's composed his masterpiece of medieval literature *'Yvain'* or *'Le Chavalier au Lion'* (*'The Knight Of The Lion'*) in which the hero Yvain (Owein) is heir to the post-Roman kingdom of Rheged in northwestern Britain once ruled by his father King  Urien, both of whom are historical figures, Owein succeeding Urien after he defeated the Anglo-Saxons in battle around 593.

 One tale has Yvain saving a lion from a dragon – hence his title 'Knight Of The Lion' – and in medieval times lions were thought to only come to life three days after they were born hence a religious connection to the resurrected Christ. Tristan, Lamorak, and Lancelot all have a rampant lion on their shields in medieval romance, and Lancelot is the knight most often connected to Lancashire. This may well be the secret behind King Richard's choice of the lion – the representation of Christ, the connection to the northern kingdoms through Rheged and Lancelot, and the numerous legendary connections.

Significant members of this order can be assembled as follows:

King Richard I Plantagenet 'The Lion Heart' (1189-1199) – Black Lion on Red.

William 'The Lion' Of Scotland, House Of Canmore (1214-1249) – Yellow Lion on Red.

Llywelyn 'The Great' (1172-1240) – Possibly Red Lion on Yellow with invected frame.

(Supported Northern Barons but married Joan daughter of King John in 1205).

William Marshall, Earl Of Pembroke (1146-1219) – Red Lion on vertically split ground of yellow left and green right.

(William became Guardian to young Henry III effectively making him King for a time).

Earl Ranulf I (Meschin), Earl of Chester (1120-1129) – Red Lion on Yellow.

Lady Dervorguilla of Galloway, held 'Cumberland' (1210-1290) – Red Lion on White.

(Daughter Of King David 1 and Matilda Of Chester).

Earl Ranulf II (de Gernons), Earl of Chester (1129-1153) – White Lion on Red.

Roger 'Hell' De Lacy / the De Lacy family – Purple Lion on Yellow.

(Probably Robyn Hoode's Commander under the Earls of Chester).

The design of the 'lion rampant' then became highly popular in medieval European countries immediately across the English Channel from London and south east England, and only later in the 13th century does the one, two, or three 'passant guardant' linear lion design known to us today become popular for royal use in England and France.

1189: In an evidently unpopular move, at some point during these activities King Richard assigns the revenues of

Derbyshire and Nottinghamshire to his brother John. This obviously has an impact on what becomes the traditional back-story for the tales of Robyn Hoode.

In turn John (at this time simply *'Count of Mortain'*) confirms the 'Hereditary Forestership' of these areas to Ralph fitz Stephen and his wife between 1189 and 1194, allowing them the chattels (property) of all robbers and poachers taken within the forest bounds. This obvious 'tightening of the law' and the 'new order' now in control of Robyn Hoode's territory evidently contributed to the outlawing of him and his followers once again as noted by Scottish writer John Major in his work on Scottish history quoted shortly.

1189-1190: *The famous 3rd Crusade takes place featuring King Richard 'Coeur-de-Lion', 'The Lion-Heart'.*

King Richard Rides Against Saladin In One Of A Tiny Number Of Contemporary Depictions, This One From 13th Century Floor Tiles Found At Chertsy Abbey.

1190: A late and somewhat local legend records that Robyn Hoode (now aged around 60) helped Reuben of Stamford and his daughter escape the historically recorded 'Massacre of the Jews' at York in 1190 giving us another date with which to enclose this period.

In the *'Garland'* tale of *'Robin Hood's Encounter With The Beggar'* Robyn decides to single-handedly charge a toll fee from a beggar of similar age to himself who passes through the area, only to be severely beaten by the beggar's pike-staff!

In the second part of the story we find the verse: *"I have been the watchman in this wood, Near hand this forty year, Yet I was never so hard bestead, As you have found me here."* This verse clearly places this story around the year 1190.

In the second part of the story two of Robyn's men then pursue the beggar who also out-smarts them and escapes, teaching them the same lesson he taught Robyn – looks can be deceiving!

The Capture Of King Richard Depicted In The 'Book In Honour Of The King & Of Sicilian Matters' By Peter Of Eboli Written In The 13th Century & Clearly Showing King Richard 3 Times As A Templar.

1193: Saladin, King Richard's heroic and chivalrous opponent, dies 28th

February 1193 out in the Holy Land.

1193-1194: Scottish writer John Major states that Robyn Hoode was outlawed (probably specifically by the Scots or Ralph fitz Stephen this time) while Richard I was held captive in Germany. It is then recorded that:

"Full thirteen yeares, and something more,
These northerne parts he vexed full sore"

This possibly takes his outlaw days up to 1207 or even to 1210 when he finally ends his courtly relationship and gets 'married' to Marian in the eyes of the church and the law (now in his 70's).

The Tudor Poet Laureate 'Skelton', in a play for Henry VIII (1509-1547) entitled *'Downfall Of The Earl Of Huntington'*, listed all the known Robyn Hoode locations up to that 16th century date by putting dialogue into the mouth of Will Scarlett. They include:

"Sherwood, Barnesdale 'shrogs', Nottingham 'red cliffs', Blythe and Tickhill (where Robyn entertained his 'guests'), Bradford (George-a-Green's home), Wakefield (home of the 'pinner'), Barnsley (home of the 'potter'), Farnsfield (where the nuns supplied napkins, shirts, and bands), Kendal (where 'Bateman' supplied 'Kendal green' cloth), Leeds (where "Sharpe' supplied arrows), Rotherham (where 'Jackson' the bowyer / bow maker lived), and Mansfield (where Scarlett and Scathelock won a wrestling match), . . ."

Skelton's work is extremely important in the study of Robyn Hoode as he had access to manuscript sources later destroyed by religious enthusiasts in the Dissolution Of The Monasteries and the English Civil War. He also had access to royal and national archive material (which he appears to have brought together in his work) and a patron in the form of Henry VIII who was extremely well read and would not have taken kindly to 'mistakes' finding their way into the final performance - a king in fact famous to history for the use of the beheading axe! Skelton's work, therefore, can be accorded a reasonable amount of certainty.

1193: *January - John concludes a treaty with King Phillip II of France and tries to seize the English throne while Richard is away on Crusade. He is stopped by Richard's Justiciars, one of which had been the powerful Northern Baron Ranulf de Glanville, 'Chief Justiciar Of England' until 1190, and Sheriff of Lancashire and Yorkshire.*

John's influence in the affairs of Sherwood and Nottingham was evidently not limited to the appointment of Hereditary Foresters. It would appear that William de Wendenal (Sheriff of Nottingham 1191-1194 and who was not apparently connected to the Earl of Chester's family) firmly supported Richard's younger brother John - hence King Richard's attack on Nottingham Castle in 1194.

Bagot's Park & The Needwood Forest Staffordshire.

At some unspecified point in his career Robyn Hoode evidently meets (or meets again), and chooses as his betrothed, 'Maid' Marian (Marmion).

Ladies play a very small part in the early tales of Robyn

Hoode and it has to be said that Marian does not appear at all in surviving written sources until over 300 years after the death of Robyn Hoode. It is wrong, however, to argue from silence that she was simply not there! The tradition must have a root source worthy of closer investigation and appears to stand on some historic foundation.

A later ballad written in the reign of Edward IV (1461-1483) says she was more beautiful than Edward's then mistress Jane Shore, but this is not a view taken by all writers.

As noted, in reality she was probably a young daughter of the 'Marmion' family who held Baggot's Park around Abbots Bromley (by Tutbury, Loxley, Doveridge, and Chartley) in the 1170s and 1180s where the couple may have first met back in the 1140s. Her nickname may have been 'Clorinda' in honour of an earlier French poem current at the time and she was probably younger than Robyn by as much as 20 years or more.

Evidently she is as good as any man, she can shoot a bow, ride, hunt, and fight – which one story has her doing for an hour when she first meets Robyn dressed as a page boy who he fails to recognize. They both get injured and Robyn asks her to join his band at which point Marian recognizes his voice from some earlier encounter (probably when they were much younger) and they then settle down together.

Women of this kind were not unique in Robyn's immediate circle – indeed in his family line. Hawise (countess) Aumale (died 1214), daughter and heiress of William (le Gros) Aumale who we have already encountered, was described by the chronicler Richard of Devises as; "*a*

Lady Dervorguilla Of Galloway.

woman who was almost a man, lacking nothing virile except the virile organs" and, as already noted, Lady Dervorguilla Of Galloway (1210-1290), daughter of King David I and Matilda Of Chester, similarly ruled parts of Southern Scotland bordering on Lancashire and Cumbria in her own right, and may have even bordered upon lands later inherited by Robyn himself at Plumpton Park and Ingleton.

Certainly by the time King Richard arrives in England on his second visit Robyn has decided to make some form of official declaration that he and Marian intend to 'marry' in the medieval sense of such a partnership.

1194: King Richard's England Visit 2 (2 months):

Richard returns to English soil for the second and last time landing at Sandwich on Sunday 20th March. By the 23rd March he's at St. Paul's, London.

Then he moves on up to Nottingham which surrenders to him after three days with its defenders seeking his mercy. By Easter he's at Northampton then eight days later Richard receives the crown from Hubert Walter (Archbishop of Canterbury) at Winchester in the presence of King William of Scotland.

On the 12th May the now fully crowned King Richard leaves Portsmouth for Normandy where he meets his brother John at Lisieux who falls at his feet seeking clemency. At this point the 'red team' of Richard beats the 'blue team' of John for the time being.

1194: 24th March to (Mid) April: During this period there is a three day siege of Nottingham Castle and Robyn Hoode (now aged around 64) meets King Richard (his junior age 36) in the surrounding forests. The two become friends and later traditionally say farewell at 'Ye Olde Trip To Jerusalem' pub at the foot of Nottingham Castle walls.

At this encounter Robyn is also granted the right to marry Marian (a type of 'pledge' or 'betrothal') and given rights to her lands at 'Malaset' in the 'Lancastrian Marches' where he settles as a Squire and servant of the crown for the next 16 years (up to 1210). Most of his younger followers then serve King Richard in his French wars, die, or settle on Robyn's lands on their return.

There exists just one contemporary pictorial depiction of King Richard's capture by Duke Leopold Of Austria in the *'Liber ad honorem Augusti sive de rebus Siculis'* (*'Book in honour of the king of Sicilian Matters'*) by Peter of Eboli, written in the early 13th century, and it shows King Richard clearly dressed as a Templar. There also appears the 'Lilly Crucifix' plant design in the hands of Emperor Henry VI of Germany to whom Duke Leopold sells Richard, a coded Templar symbol that also appears on the Great Seal of Richard. Evidently Richard's divine authority in this respect has now been passed to his captor Emperor Henry VI. Now we know which order King Richard supported we can return to Robyn Hoode and the vows he would have taken in order to follow Richard and join the 'red team'.

In Tennyson's *'The Idylls Of The King'* the knights of the Round Table swear an oath which essentially crystallizes that sworn by the orders of knights throughout the Crusades:

To break the heathen and uphold the Christ,
To ride abroad redressing human wrongs,
To speak no slander, no, nor listen to it,

To honour his own words as if his God's,
To lead sweet lives in purest chastity,
To love one maiden only, cleave to her
And worship her by years of noble deeds,
Until they won her . . .

1196: As noted, in this year the historically recorded figure Robert (Fitz) Odo, Lord of Loxley Manor in Staffordshire, is recorded as *'dispossessed'* and spends a year as an outlaw robber until Richard restores his lands.

1198: King Richard passes a law against poaching in the royal forests such that the killing of a deer would result in *"the removal of the offender's eyes and testicles"*! This actually made it more of a young man's 'game' or 'tournament' rather than preventing it.

Nottinghamshire Woodland Winter Sunset.

1199: *On the 6ᵗʰ April King Richard dies from a crossbow wound while besieging Chaluz Castle in France.*

1199: This genuine entry is contained in the *Royal Court Rolls* for the *County Of Cumberland*, for the month of May, in the year 1199, in the reign of King Richard I called 'Lion Heart', and is here translated in full from the Medieval Latin:

"Ric (Richard) *son of Troite appeals* (legally complains against) *Rob de Holdelme. Because he* (Rob) *wickedly deserted his Lord King Henry* (Henry II King of England 1154-1189) *and broke his fealty to him, and laid waste to his land, and besieged his city and castle, and allied himself to the King of Scotland* (William The Lion 1165-1214), *the mortal enemy of King Henry, to his* (the King's) *harm."*

"And for this, as he (Ric) *says, he appealed* (accused) *him* (Rob) *before the same king outside the town of Geddington. Because he did not dare at that time to defend himself in the King's Court, nor did he wish to, therefore King Henry banished* (outlawed) *Rob from his Court. And if he, Rob, wishes to deny this, he* (Richard) *offers to prove it by body or by free man of his* (choosing) (i.e. trial by combat between Richard and Robyn). *Rob comes and defends the felony word by word, as a man of sixty years or more, or by his son* (on his behalf)."

"Ric (Richard), *being asked before which justices he made that appeal in the days of King Henry II, says it was before the King himself, and he neither produces or names any justice or other before whom the dispute was tried."*

"Rob (Robyn) *comes and says that at the time Ric says, that he, Rob, was with the King of Scotland besieging the Castle of Carlisle, Udard, Rob's father, was seized of the land of* ...(land not listed), *which he* (now) *claims against the same Ric* (who has evidently taken this land from Rob's father Udard). *And* (while) *in the service of King Henry within the said castle, there he* (Ric) *seized thereof* (and at that time Rob held not land), *and he* (Rob) *puts himself under oath of lawful men of that county. And that this appeal was made* (by Richard) *through spite, to disinherit him. And a day is given to them, 15 days from St Luke's day, to hear their judgment."*

"Afterwards it was considered that since that time the said Ric had concealed this dispute for so long his appeal fails, and he remains in mercy. And Rob is quit (i.e. Robyn is pardoned by the justices of King Richard I the Lion Heart and found 'not guilty' of the accusation of desertion. His father's lands would then be returned to him).

This whole entry is interesting as this Rob (Robyn) de Holdelme (Hode / Ode) is the right age at 68-69 and already apparently has one son of reasonable years (who the legal wording implies shared the same name as his father, slightly confusing the Justiciars).

His father's name is also given as Udard (de Holdelme) a knight who served under King Henry II during the unsuccessful Scottish siege of Carlisle Castle for three months in 1173.

It would be nice to think that we had finally found mention of the real Robyn Hoode.

Sunset Over Cumberland.

The Reign Of King John (1199-1216)

1199-1216: *On the 27th May King John ('Lackland' or 'Softsword') is crowned King Of England at Westminster Abbey. In 1200 he concludes the 'Treaty Of Le Goulet' accepting Philip II as his overlord in Normandy and the Angevin territory on condition that Philip accepts*

John as King Of England. The treaty breaks down and wars in France continue.

1199: King John grants the Upper Derwent estate (most of the Ronksley Valley) to the White Canons of Welbeck Abbey, perhaps in the hope of quelling the outlaws there, a similar move tried elsewhere with the Black Canons of the Augustinian / Cistercian Order. Some Abbots even had their own 'foresters' and 'courts' at this time.

However the austere Premonstratensian White Canons hated the 'liberal' Black Canons as much as the outlaws did and the outlaws and White Cannons appear to have got on rather well. It is even possible that Robyn had one of his camps in the remote valley of 'Abbey Brook' behind their Abbey at Welbeck.

1199: Some tales concern earlier visits of Robyn to London, often with a desire to audience with the queen.

The two primary *'Garland'* tales are *'Robin Hood And Queen Katherine'* and *'Robin Hood's Chase'*. These stories have caused a great deal of confusion down the years as 'the queen' is always consistently given as 'Katherine' and no likely contender can be found anywhere in the Medieval period!

The first royal 'Katherine' to appear is during the reign of Henry VIII (1509-1547) when Robin Hood stories were incredibly popular and versions of these stories from this period still survive. Even more confusing we also have three 'Catherine's' to go at; Catherine Of Aragon, Catherine Howard, and Catherine Parr, all wives of Henry VIII. This is all simply a distraction!

Taking the name 'Katherine' and searching only the period of Robyn's life between 1130 and 1220 we have another strong contender – St Katherine of Alexandria.

The cult of St Katherine was one of the strongest to develop during the life-time of Robyn Hoode. While there is no actual evidence that she really existed, she was reportedly born of a wealthy or royal family in Alexandria and defended Christianity against the Roman tyrant Maximin (C.278-312) who was eventually defeated by the famous Christian Roman Emperor (and 'Yorkshire man') Constantine 'The Great' at the Battle of the Milvian Bridge.

The Medieval legend (which interests us here) made her entirely a royal queen as a daughter of King Costus of Cyprus. As a teenage virgin she rejects the advances of Maximin, defeats Maximin's philosophers with skilful arguments, is tortured on a wheel which breaks before harming her so she is beheaded instead (hence she is sometimes depicted holding a sword) and her body is miraculously transferred to Mount Sinai where it was then reported as rediscovered around the year 800. She is depicted with a sword on the Norman font in Bakewell Church, Derbyshire, which dates to the period just before Robyn Hoode.

Her relics then began to appear in Europe during the 11th and 12th centuries. Rouen Monastery in Rouen, the capital city of Normandy, claimed to have Katherine's fingers, and Westminster Abbey claimed a phial of oil from her body brought back from Mount Sinai by Edward the Confessor (the last Anglo Saxon king 1042-1066). The University of Paris, founded in the middle of the 12th century, claimed her as their saint, Canterbury and York also had strong connections to the cult, with York Minster still retaining her story depicted in the stained glass of the nave to this day.

Many local shrines spread across Britain and France throughout the 12th century and several late medieval pilgrimage narratives have survived (including John Mandeville in the 14th century and Felix Fabri in the 15th century), then Katherine was one of the saints who famously spoke to Joan of Arc.

In 'Robin Hood And Queen Katherine' the queen sends her page

'Richard Partington' (probably Sir Richard of Partington, a town now in Trafford, Greater Manchester) to Nottingham to find Robyn and invite him to an archery contest in London that is obviously based on the one which appears in 'A Lyttell Geste Of Robyn Hode' and other stories. The contest includes Tepus, Clifton, Woodcock, and the Bishop of Hereford for the king, and Sir Richard Lea, Will Scarlet, Midge the Miller's son, and Little John for the queen.

The story then continues in 'Robin Hood's Chase' with Robyn winning the contest and the king deciding to chase him north:

> "What though his pardon granted was,
> While he with him did stay;
> Yet, after, the king was angry with him,
> When he was gone his way."

The king comes to Nottingham, Sherwood, and through Yorkshire, causing Robyn to flee to Newcastle, on to Berwick, across to Carlisle and to Lancaster at the advice of Little John, then down to Chester, where the king also eventually turns up. Meanwhile Robyn returns to London and Queen Katherine claiming he is there to see the king who returns after spending three weeks away searching for Robyn and realizes he has been fooled, Robyn has already returned north and Katherine insists that his pardon is upheld.

This king would have to be King John and John effectively had two real life 'Queens' who may fit the bill as the 'Queen Katherine' of the story.

He first married the teenage Isabella, Countess of Gloucester, in 1189 when she was around 16, but obtained an annulment of the marriage upon becoming King ten years later in 1199 as they were half-second cousins (great grandchildren of Henry I) and technically prohibited from marrying under the medieval laws of consanguinity. As King Henry II himself had betrothed them before his death Pope Clement III granted a special dispensation for them to marry but forbade sexual relations which inevitably resulted in no children.

As the 'virgin queen' resisting a 'tyrant king' for ten years it is just possible that she was popularly thought of in the same vein as St Katherine in the years between 1189 and 1199 and the presence of both the king and queen in the Robyn Hoode story narrows the time-period down to 1199 when she was effectively 'jilted' or 'dumped' before the end of August after John's coronation on the 27th May.

Whether history records it or not, it is not inconceivable that the newly crowned King John chose to travel around his Baron's northern domains for three weeks rallying support (as in the story) before taking his fight to France for the closing months of 1199.

Isabella also illustrates the problem with names and 'nick-names' very well as she is known as Isabel, Joan, Eleanor, (and frequently Hadwisa, Hawisia, Hawise, Avise, and Avisa all meaning 'Countess'), as well as Isabella.

It is not a great leap to speculate that she entered the Robyn Hoode legends as a 'type' of the by now highly popular virgin 'St Katherine' or 'Queen Katherine'.

She married again twice after John and died in 1217.

John then married a second Isabella 'of Angouleme' in 1200 who is his Queen until his death in 1216 when she replaces the crown lost in the Wash with her own circlet and crowns her nine year old son King Henry III, placing him into the care of William Marshall. At this time Isabella's seal shows a slender medieval lady in a long flowing cloak holding a Templar cross topped by a peacock in her left hand, and another 'lily crucifix' in her right.

She then returns to France to marry Hugh X of Lusignan "le Brun" to whom she had been betrothed before marrying John. As an alternative Hugh had been offered the hand of Isabella's eldest daughter Joan but, upon seeing that Isabella's beauty had not diminished, he married her as originally envisaged in 1220 and her daughter 'Princess Joan' then married King Alexander II of Scotland in 1221.

Isabella of Angouleme is anything but 'virginal' producing a total of 14 children and is unlikely to be the 'Queen Katherine' of the story. But there is clearly no reason why it couldn't be Isabella, Countess of Gloucester.

1202: *The 4th Crusade takes place which includes many children. Europe is running out of male nobility and many widowed women with noble inheritance start to join the Crusading orders as 'knights' in their own right. Constantinople is captured and a Latin Empire established.*

1204-1215: *1st April 1204 Eleanor Of Aquitaine dies. John confiscates English lands from Norman barons who take sides with Philip II, which*

includes most of the Northern Barons who formerly supported King Richard.

Eventually there is a two year peace from 1206-1208 - but John falls out of favour with Pope Innocent III who pulls his Bishops out of Britain in 1209, excommunicating John in November.

John then makes peace with King William 'The Lion' of Scotland, and again in 1209 when he marches an army to Norham near Berwick, marries King William's daughters to English nobles and William's son Alexander to his own eldest daughter Joan.

He then asserts his authority over Ireland in 1210, makes peace with Llewelyn The Great of Wales in 1211, and ends his quarrel with the Pope in 1213. John is then fighting in France throughout 1214. Meanwhile the Northern Barons continue to revolt and plot to kill the king (1212-1215).

1210-1213: Despite the personal blessing of the union by King Richard I, it is likely that Robyn Hoode finally 'marries' Marian under the great yew tree in the church yard at St Cuthbert's Church, Doveridge, in the middle of the six years during which all church services in England and Wales were banned by Pope Innocent III.

This would explain why the already existing wooden or stone structure of the medieval church at Doveridge (which still survives in use to this day) could not be used for the occasion.

The ancient yew tree would already have been over 800 years old (surviving from at least 400AD) and magnificent in Robyn's time, providing an obvious alternative out-door venue for a collection of forester knights.

It is highly possible that the couple already had children, including a son (possibly two) and daughter, by this time. Marriage was a far more 'fluid' institution in medieval times than it is now. There was also the concept, prevalent amoung knights especially, of 'courtly love' in which the lady was 'viewed from a-far off' and 'courted' for as long as possible without an actual marriage ceremony taking place – the courtly love of the romances. This was a kind of perpetual 'engagement' with a greater element of permanence than today.

As noted it is highly probable that Robyn knew Marion from his local area around Loxley, Doveridge, Abbott's Bromley, Bagot's Park, Tutbury, and Chartley, and that a measure of family life ('courtly love') had begun during Robyn's outlaw years - even before the blessing of King Richard I. The relatively late 18th century tale *'Robin Hood And Maid Marian'* puts it this way:

> *"But fortune bearing these lovers a spite,*
> *That soon they were forced to part;*
> *To the merry green wood then went Robin Hood,*
> *With a sad and sorrowful heart."*

Eventually Marian goes to Robin disguised as a page boy and they sword fight equally matched till Robin asks the 'boy' to join his band and Marian reveals who she is. While this story is just another variant of the 'matched conflict' plot, it does support a separation of Robyn and Marian from youth to adulthood and it is evident that the later 'wedding' at Doverirdge was mostly undertaken for the benefit of legality, legitimacy and the requirements of the medieval church.

We can also identify from surviving pertinent medieval records that 'Sir' Roger (Friar) of Tutbury (or Titbury) would have most likely been the incumbent who presided at the wedding. Roger came from the magnificent Tutbury Abbey Church founded by the Ferrers family next to their castle, both of which remain to this day.

> "Yet to fair Marian bound he stood,
> And love's debt paid her duly.
> Whom curb of strictest law could not hold in,
> Love with obeyedness and a wink could win."

(Love song 'The Rival Archer' from Jones's "Musical Dream" published 1606).

Some authorities would write Marian out of the story altogether, arguing that she does not appear in early surviving tales, however a connection exists between a 'Robin' and a 'Marian' in the French May Festivities going back into the 13th century which could just as well have crossed the English Channel from England as migrated back the other way to 'infect' the legends of Robyn Hoode. Simply too much evidence exists to write Maid Marian out of the original story.

1210-1217: At some point during these years it is possible that some event occurs in Robyn's life to draw his attention to

higher things as there survives a very late and rare legend which indicates a return to Robyn's religious roots.

The Ancient Yew Tree At St Cuthbert's Church, Doveridge.

It is highly possible that, despite obviously being much younger than Robyn, Marian has passed away from disease, or in child birth, or followed the traditions of 'courtly love' and chosen to retire to a monastic life, or even, as legend would have it, been poisoned at the instruction of King John before his death (see a later section), leaving Robyn her estates. This may have led to the mistaken use of 'Lancashire' as the location for the geography which follows in *'Robin Whood Turned Hermit'* by a writer obviously unfamiliar with the material they were working with - 'Depe-Dale' is in fact in Derbyshire!

"To Depe-Dale come, most wisely Robin Whood,
Surveys each Nook and Corner of the Wood

At length he finds a lonely rocky cell,
And in Devotion there resolves to dwell,"

Robin Whood Turned Hermit (Francis Peck 1735).

A single manuscript survives of a story entitled *'Robin Whood Turned Hermit'* in a collection of ballads made by the Stamford antiquary Francis Peck and dated very late in the Robyn Hoode tradition at 1735. Peck thought that *"This song is, I think, designed in a true Manner."* He thought it contained genuine material from an earlier age even though heavily polluted by later additions. His assertion of authenticity rings true as his summary of the story includes material not found anywhere else. Robyn moves his force:

"At last coming to Lyndric a famous hill near Dale Abbey in Lancashire (as noted actually it's in Derbyshire) Robin Whood falls asleep and hath a strange Dream there. Which at his awaking, he relates to his Companions, and then tells them, that he is resolved forthwith to retire, and to turn Hermit."

He dismisses and advises the group of his usual named followers then: *"Robin retires to Depe Dale, chuses the penitent Thief for his Patron, and spends the Remainder of his Time in great Penance and Devotion."* **Then, in this story as in others, he eventually feels ill and goes to a place named 'Kirklees'.**

Intriguingly there was indeed an anonymous outlaw recorded in a chronicle of the foundation of Dale Abbey by Thomas of Muskham in the 13th century, and Muskham placed the outlaw in the reign of Henry II (1154-1189) when the whole area between the river Derwent and river Erewash was royal forest.

In this original source we are not told if the anonymous outlaw was *'Robin Whood'* but the story of the dream followed by repentance is essentially the same. Is this an original story of Robyn later embellished, or a story 'high jacked' and transformed by an 18th century antiquarian – we may never know for sure?

The Hermitage At Dale Abbey Derbyshire.

1215: It is said by some that Robyn Hoode (by now aged around 85) marched south under the banners of the Northern Barons to face King John. History then records the rest:

1215: *On the 6th January John interviews the restless Barons in London. 4th March he takes the oath as a Crusader but, despite this 'nod' to knighthood, on the 12th May Civil War breaks out with dissident Barons occupying London by the 17th May.*

The following month 15th June John seals the famous charter at Runnymede, makes peace with the Barons on the 19th June, and meets them again at Oxford 16th July. However, in September a Papal bull annuls the charter and Civil War starts all over again with John capturing Rochester 11th October and campaigning in northern and eastern England in December.

The head of the regional party and family group in which Robyn would have traveled to London would have been William de Fortibus, Earl of Albemarle (Aumale), a group which would also have included the man effectively 'Robyn Hoode's Hereditary Boss' John de Lacy, Lord of Pontefract Castle (Wakefield, West Yorkshire), Northern Baron Richard de Percy, Robert de Roos, Lord of Hamlake Castle (Helmsley, North Yorkshire), Roger de Montbegon, Lord of Hornby Castle (Lancashire), Henry de

Bohun and Richard de Clare (of Hereford), and Eustace de Vesci, Lord of Alnwick Castle (Northumberland).

Other northern signatories to the charter at Runnymede included Llewelyn the Great (King of Wales) and Alexander II (King Of Scotland), along with Brother Aymeric, Master of the Knights Templar in England, and Master Pandulff, sub-deacon and member of the Papal Household representing the Pope.

Interestingly, despite 12 prominent southern and Irish Bishops and 20 Abbots signing Magna Carta, none of the northern Bishops or Abbots signed!

The Charter signed at Runnymede did not apply to Chester as it was a separate feudal domain at this time so Earl Ranulf de Blunderville was notably missing from the group of Northern Barons. Earl Ranulf actually granted his very own Magna Carta around this time, with some articles similar to those found in King John's Runnymede Charter.

A late 17th century tale entitled *'Robin Hood And The Valliant Knight'* appears to sit most comfortably in these days of the Baron's Revolt and Civil War.

1215: In the story the king finally gets fed up with Robyn and his men harassing his bishops and noble peers and calls a summer *"council of state, to know best what is to be done."* It is decided that a trusty and worthy knight named 'Sir William' (who, frankly, could be anybody!) should take a hundred armored bowmen with spears north on mid-summer's day and capture Robyn.

A week later, on the last day of June, Sir William finds Robyn and offers terms of surrender based on the King's letter of instruction which Robyn declines. The two teams of equally matched archers then line up and let fly and 'Sir William' is killed in the first flight. The battle lasts all morning until mid-day with the King's archers returning to London later that day without prejudice. Robyn returns to the green wood and is

taken ill leading to his desire to be bled by a monk (who kills him). Robyn's men then scatter to Flanders, France, Spain, and Rome, with only a few returning later.

Evidently Robyn returns home in time for Mid-Summer's Day in June 1215 and leads the archers stand-off being now too old to resort to hand-to-hand combat. They win and this failure to resolve the problem of Robyn Hoode may have been a contributing factor to the king himself heading north six months later.

On the 24th December 1215 King John is in residence at Nottingham Castle with the Sheriff Philip Marc (1214-1224) while on his last campaign north to defeat dissident Northern Barons and meet with the forces of Alexander II King of Scotland above Berwick in late January 1216.

What is important to our narrative is that Martin Parker writes, in his 'A True Tale Of Robin Hood' (1632), that Robyn fires an arrow into Nottingham containing a note which pledges allegiance in return for forgiveness. While the lords and king are debating what to do about this over two thirds of Robyn's outlaws "... *fled away, Unto the Scottish king;*" rather than risk the out-come. In the Irish Ballad 'Robin Hood And The Scotsman' (printed 1796) a Scottish archer called 'Sawney' is actually recorded as being enlisted in Robyn's archers and is probably not alone.

Sadly the debate about Robyn's note never reaches an out-come as Robyn dies before forgiveness comes. The same is also true of the king.

1216: *The 18th of May sees John's fleet scattered in a storm and Prince Louis of France (son of King Philip II, to whom the Pope had 'given' England) lands safely in England and joins the dissident Barons. On*

5th June John pulls out of Winchester into western England from where he fights the rebels in the midlands during September.

What happens next is still not altogether clear.

According to the official version of the story, on a march up the east coast, John famously loses the royal treasure in the Wash (the *'Wellstream'* or 'Old River Ouse' between King's Lynn and Newark) and pulls back to Swineshead Abbey where he drowns his sorrows on 'peaches and new cider', then on to Sleaford to the west and the Bishop Of Lincoln's Castle at Newark where he dies after three days unknown illness (some authorities say possibly dysentery as the result of gluttony) on the 18th October 1216, aged just 48. His embalmed body is then sent for burial at Worcester Cathedral.

Victorian Photo Of Newark Castle.

John's route has always looked suspicious and other versions of the story imply that the treasure had already been used to pay off either the Scots or John's Mercenaries. He also owed a vast sum of money to the Knights Templar and many authorities think that the sinking baggage train was simply a cover story or that there was no treasure in the carts to lose! Contemporary sources sometimes limit the 'treasure' to just items of church furnishings.

A 13th century story in circulation very soon after his death told that John tried to steal church treasure from Swineshead Abbey, killing the beloved Abbot with a single sword blow when he tried to prevent it, and was consequently poisoned on purpose by the (probably Templar) monks.

There is then the mystery of why he turned to the west and headed in land for Newark? Could he have been trying to reach his palace lodge at Wellow, immediately north of the river Trent and now known as 'King's Clipstone', to seek urgent medical attention, but died at Newark on the way? To some extent this would better fit the facts.

Clipstone From The 'Antiquities Of Nottinghamshire'.

The Reign Of King Henry III (1216-1272)

1216-1272: *Henry III Plantagenet takes the throne.*

1216-1218: Represents the probable death period of our Robyn Hoode I (Senior) around the age of 86-88. And, true to form,

there are then at least four possible burial sites.

The earliest burial site recorded in any of the surviving written legends is in 'Skelton's play for Henry VIII (written before 1547) in a wish Robyn makes to be buried:

"... at Wakefield, underneath the abbey wall;"

... and this is further recorded in the play as ratified by a decree made by King John (probably actually some kind of 'foundation charter' of some kind passed before his unexpected death).

The problem is - there are no known actual 'Abbey' ruins surviving in central Wakefield today!

Possible Burial Site Number One

The closest actual 'Abbey' Church to Wakefield's medieval town centre is Kirkstall Abbey – which is actually a considerable distance away near Leeds.

Its founder, Henry de Lacy, is frequently connected to Robyn Hoode, it had direct connections to Fountains Abbey where Robyn's relics ended up, it was developed within the lifetime of Robyn (being founded on the 19th May 1147 at Barnoldswick), it resides within the area of Leeds ('Lees'), and it was formerly a Saxon church set in woodland clearings named 'Kirk-stoel' meaning simply 'Church-place'.

Is it therefore the real source of the 'Kirk-Lees' of later stories?

The surviving ruins are truly magnificent and well worth a

visit – but Robyn Hoode has never been connected to this site by anyone! It certainly ranks as a high possibility and attention needs to be given to any surviving burial records on this site relating to the medieval noble families named in this book – but there may be a better site:

Possible Burial Site Number Two

Another candidate may be Nostell Priory based solely on its location in the village of Wragby between Doncaster and Wakefield. It is the largest foundation in the Wakefield catchment area to have any possible connections to the Robyn of this book.

Nostell Priory was a 12th century Augustinian foundation with Templar connections dedicated to St Oswald and supported

initially by Robert de Lacy of Pontefract, Thurstan of York, William I Foliot, and later by King David of Scotland in the days of Robyn Hoode. 'Aldulf', confessor to King Henry I (1100-1135), was the first known prior in about 1114 strengthening royal connec- tions, and the king appears enthroned on the earliest surviving priory seal. Sadly all traces of the priory above ground have disappeared.

During some digging in ages past a stone box coffin with a carved lid was discovered and taken to the Victorian Wragby Church which now stands close by the site. The design on the coffin lid is the distinctive forester / Templar knight cross we have come to recognize as associated with Robyn and forester sites all over the region.

This may be the most likely Monastic Foundation closest to

Wakefield and still under construction in Robyn's territory at the time of Robyn's death, in which case the real Robyn Hoode may lie buried somewhere under the grass meadow which now covers the ruins. Traveling to Wakefield from his forest realms Robyn would frequently have passed this location. The site is owned by the National Trust and open to the public but no historic associations to Robyn Hoode have ever been documented at this site either.

Nostell Priory House As It Appears Today.

Possible Burial Site Number Three

In order to find the burial site of the real Robyn Hoode we need to locate the monastic structure that would have been regarded as 'Wakefield Abbey' by Robyn himself in around 1210-1220, and would have still been under construction at that date for him to be capable of being buried under its walls.

For Wakefield (*'Wachfield'*) to have two churches and three priests when the Domesday Survey was compiled in 1086 means it was a big place and would have remained so into the days of

Robyn Hoode, hence why he would want to be buried there. It was certainly a regional centre – if not the equivalent to a small medieval 'city' capitol to the area. The two originally Saxon foundations were probably the sites Robyn had in mind when he specified *'Wakefield'* and would have been being converted into stone by the Normans in the 12th century, probably between 1150 and 1250, a process Robyn himself had contributed to in Whitby and Barnsdale.The main church in Wakefield is now known as the 'Cathedral Church of All Saints' right in the centre of the original Medieval town, 'All Saints' as it has an altar in each wing dedicated to a different saint making four of them in all. 'All Saints' also often means that its original dedication has been lost. It is thought to stand on the site of one of the early Saxon churches recorded in the Domesday Survey.

Archaeological work below floor level in 2013 revealed the plan of the smaller original Medieval Church with at least three burials formerly under carved stone lids close to the altar end. These burials have been carbon dated to the late Saxon / early medieval period, virtually contemporary with the life of our Robyn Hoode.

One Of Three Early Medieval Burials Discovered In Wakefield Cathedral In 2013. (Courtesy Of Wessex Archaeology).

Although history books place the building of the main church to 1349, around 1220 (the period of Robyn's death) the original stone church south isle was under construction with the recent archaeology appearing to back this up. No further excavation was permitted, the new floor was set in place, and, if this is the 'Abbey' he had in mind, the body of the real Robyn Hoode was entombed again for future generations to discover. Ironically he would probably now be below the new polished wood 'lower altar table' which is in the shape of a giant Templar cross!

However, while this is now certainly thought to be one of the two churches recorded in the Domesday Book back in 1086, none of the patrons, known burials, land holders, or main phases of building construction yet conclusively matches evidence for connections to Robyn Hoode.

English Woodland Outside Wakefield.

The other church mentioned in the Domesday Survey can almost certainly be ruled out as it is thought to be the one associated with Sandal Castle and almost certainly private. The castle was being developed in the 12th century and it is recorded that work on a northern motte, also existing at that time, was stopped as a result, however most of those responsible for Sandal Castle were avid supporters of King John.

Although there is some certainty that the intended burial site in Wakefield would have been under the 'Cathedral Church of All Saints', it has to be admitted that the picture is further confused by the fact that there were possibly as many as a dozen or more 'Chantry Chapels' in Wakefield at various times, including the famous one on the medieval town bridge and several south of the river (e.g. St Catherine's to the east), any one of which may be the burial site Robyn had in mind. As we have noted, the medieval shrines of St Catherine (Katherine), which started developing all over Europe and the UK in the 1100s, have possibly been associated with Robyn in the original medieval legends. However, this fact alone is not sufficient to point to a burial site for Robyn Hoode.

We can only hope that Robyn himself had the one recently excavated by Wessex Archaeology at the 'Cathedral Church of All Saints' in the centre of Wakefield in mind.

If the play by Skelton is ignored altogether there are equally prominent regional monastic foundations at: Doncaster (Greyfriars and Whitefriars), Roche (Abbey), Ecclesfield (Priory), Hampole (Priory), Kirklees (Priory), Monk Bretton (Priory), and Tickhill (Austin Friary and Priory).

Burial Site Number Four – The Antiquarian Fake:

In later legends Kirklees Priory takes center stage - but it is worth a closer critical look at this supposedly "traditional" legend and the site associated with it.

Robyn Hoode's death is covered by a damaged fragment containing just 27 verses in the *'Percy Folio'*, but the wording here is crucial. The section opens with Robyn declaring that he will visit *"Church Lees"* not 'Kirklees'. The surviving story goes:

1217: He meets an old woman kneeling on a plank over dark water 'banning' (assumed to mean 'cursing') Robyn Hoode. The next section is missing and we do not know what exchange took place between the pair or why she had selected Robyn as her target.

We rejoin the story where Robyn is arguing that he has nothing to fear from the prioress there (location missing) as she is his cousin. However it can be inferred that Robyn is intending to head for a priory or nunnery of some kind. Robyn arrives, the bleeding begins, Robyn realizes his cousin's treachery and notifies Little John, then the next section is again missing.

In the last surviving section Robyn fights and kills 'Red Roger', spares the prioress, and commands Little John to bury him:

"And set my bright sword at my head,
My arrows at my feet.
And lay my yew-bow by my side,
My met-yard (measuring-rod) wi..."

The end of the manuscript is then missing depriving us of the rest of Robyn's last words.

Martin Parker's 'A True Tale Of Robin Hood' (1632) contains a slightly different version. In this story it is the loss of his men that sends Robyn on a downward spiral that makes him head for a nunnery to be bled. Here it is a *"faithless friar"* that leaves Robyn to bleed out in revenge for Robyn's attitude to the clergy, then the prioress has him buried *"... in a mean case, Close by the highway side."* and places a stone there with an (unspecified) epitaph which had been "known for a hundred years" in Parker's time.

A combination of both of these stories could form the complete legend of his death, but it is interesting to note that Parker could only date the epitaph stone known in his time to around 1530.

Moving to the traditional tale, according to *'The Life & Ballads Of Robin Hood'* Robin retired to Kirklees Nunnery (Priory) in Yorkshire which is run by his kinswoman (cousin), but is bled to death by treachery initiated by Sir Roger Of Doncaster (Red Roger) and dies on the: *"18th November 1247 (the 31st year of King Henry III)"*.

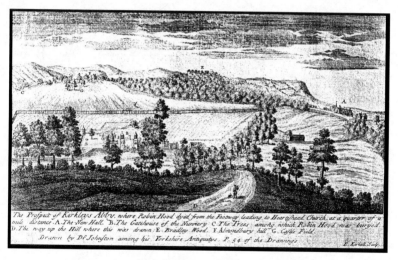

18th Century Kirklees Priory, Robin Hood's Grave Marked 'C' Far Left.

This is plainly the wrong date as Robyn would be in the region of 117 years old by now!!! However, rather than being entirely invented, it could be an honest mis-reading of *"the 1st year of King Henry III"* (1217) recorded by an earlier source now lost. Given all the facts so far examined this would certainly fit the chronology.

Sir Roger Of Doncaster (Red Roger) may have wanted Robyn

dead as he represented a knight who had risen to his position by underhanded means, secular maneuverings, and a king's appointment, rather than the usual route as a warrior monk of the Augustinian or Cistercian orders. There is also the possibility that Roger was a relative through Robyn's half-sister with his eyes on inheritance (see the family tree later in this book).

Turning to the traditional venue - Kirklees Priory was a Cistercian Nunnery dedicated to the Virgin Mary and St James founded by Reiner le Fleming, Lord of the manor of Walh-upon-Dearne, in 1155 (however some other authorities say before 1138). These are known as 'Bernardines' after Bernard of Clairvaux, 'White Monks', and were often directly connected to the Knights Templar, Bernard being the religious head of the Templars at its foundation. Sadly at this time it is not known who was the 'Prioress' or 'Abbess' of Kirklees Nunnery (Priory) around the year 1217 (or even in 1247). This could give us another relative or family name connected to Robyn but it is difficult to find any authentic connections to Robyn Hoode at all at this site.

Turning back to the oldest surviving version of *'Robyn Hoode His Death'*, those 27 fragmented verses at the end of the Percy Folio (C1650), as noted Robyn actually says that he will have his blood let at *"Church Lees"*. While it is true to say that 'Kirk' means 'Church' this is not the name of a place but a structure! The place is then also referred to as 'Lees' simply meaning 'woodland clearings' giving us the "Woodland Church" or "Church in a Woodland Clearing" or "Church-In-The-Woods" which, frankly, could be anywhere!

According to most late traditional tales Robyn is then buried alongside a nearby road, about a bow-shot from the Nunnery, under a modern stone of the 1840s which reads:

"Here under this little stone,
Lies Robert, Earl of Huntingdon,
Ne'er archer were as he so good,

And people called him Robin Hood,
Such outlaws as he and his men,
Will England never see again.
Obiit 24 kal. Decembris 1247."

The earliest record of this inscription is in the *'True Tale Of Robin Hood'* by Martin Parker published in 1632 and given an earliest known date by Parker of around 1530, but Gough's *'Sepulchral Monuments'* says the inscription *"was never on it"*! The language is entirely wrong for the period of Robyn Hoode and Nathaniel Johnstone's drawing of 'the grave' in 1665 shows quite different detail more in keeping with a Medieval tomb, so different is this that it is unclear if this is even the same grave?

Nathaniel Johnstone's drawing of the grave of
'Robard Hude' in 1665.

According to Richard Grafton in his *'Chronicle'* of 1562, Robyn was buried beside the road *"where he used to rob and spoil those that passed that way"* and upon his grave were *"the names of Robert Hood, William of Goldesborough, (Thomas?) and others were graven ...*

And at either end of the said tomb was erected a cross of stone, which is to be seen at this present (1562)." This is clearly a description of the tomb shown by Nathaniel Johnstone.

If we look closer at the relationship between the remains of Kirklees Priory and the traditional grave site there, the gatehouse where Robyn is said to have died is at least 650 yards (almost 580 meters) away to the south. It would take a huge leap of faith to believe that a man in his 80's could draw a yew longbow after having been almost bled to death and loose an arrow over a distance of 650 yards! So his actual grave, if it is located here, probably lies 'a bow-shot' between the two points which would include all the Priory itself and most of the surrounding cemetery.

Robin Hood's Grave At Kirklees C.1850.

In 1786 Richard Gough was sceptical about the grave slab in his *'Sepulchral Monuments'* and records that: *"The late Sir Samuel Armitage, owner of the premises, caused the ground under to be dug a yard deep, and found it had never been disturbed; so that it was probably brought from some other place, and by vulgar tradition ascribed to Robin Hood."* Or, in other words, they dug and didn't

even find evidence of a hole!

The traditional date of Robyn's death in '1247' is first recorded by Scottish writer John Major in 1521 and his source is unknown and the first inscribed stone at the grave site can only be dated back to the 1530s. Thomas Gale, Dean of York, invented the famous 'epitaph' in 1702 based on Martin Parker's 1632 poem *'The True Tale Of Robin Hood'*. The tomb stone (medieval coffin lid) shown in Nathaniel Johnstone's drawing of 1665 must have been moved there from another location and the 'inscription' of the famous poem is a fake from the 1840s.

In the final analysis this is the least likely burial site for the real Robyn Hoode and appears to be a very late attempt to support 17th and 18th century antiquarian views by constructing a Robin Hood 'folly' on private land for the pleasure of all concerned. This site also still remains privately owned, can not be visited, and the relatively modern 'grave' structure is currently in a state of disrepair.

Robin Hood's Grave Folly At Kirklees Priory.

1218: *The 5th Crusade, is followed by the 6th (1228), 7th (1239), and 8th (1240), none successful.*

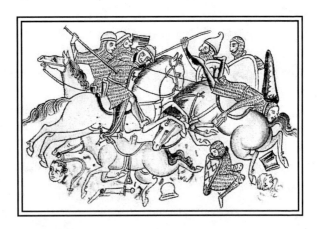

1222: *The situation around the Mediterranean is further exasperated as Mongol forces start to make incursions into Southern Europe which are*

followed up by a full scale invasion of South Eastern Europe in 1241.

The Story Continues Beyond The Original Robyn Hoode

1210-1295: Robin Hood (II) son of Robyn Hoode. It appears Robyn and Marian had already produced a daughter and a son (or two), probably some time before 1210.

A few tantalizingly brief references actually exist in pertinent medieval records and hint at the developing family of 'Hoode' in the northern counties. For example, one 'Robert Hode', a tenant of the archbishopric of York, fled the jurisdiction of the King's justices at York in 1225 and may be the original Robyn's son. Certainly the 13th century sees an explosion of the name 'Robin Hood' and its various forms, a type of expansion which would certainly place the originator somewhere back in the 12th century or before as already noted. If we re-examine some of the later tales we may possibly find fragments of the son's life compounded into them by later writers.

Based on the evidence contained in various versions of the *'Lyttell Geste'*, Robin Hood (junior) is probably alive early in the reign of Henry III (1216-1272) and at the time of the Battle Of Evesham (1265), at which point he is pardoned and in the service of King Edward I (1272-1307) for 15 months until he and his men run out of money.

A verse in the *'Geste'* reads: *"In Nottingham dwelt our comely king, well more than half a year; Yet could not hear of Robin Hood, Or in what county he were."* and we know from historical records that this could only apply to the historically recorded stay of King Edward I.

"He took out the broad seal,
And soon he let him see:

Robin knew his courtesy,
And set him on his knee:"
Robin Hood And The King (From 'Robin Hood's Garland' 1670).

After king's service Robin (II) returns to the family chapel at Barnsdale in the green-wood and is 'seduced' by the forest to return there for a further 22 years taking his life up to around 1295. He probably dies aged in his 80's just like his father.

Ancient Trees In Barnsdale Forest.

It is certainly possible that later compilers of the Robyn Hoode tales have mixed together more than one strand of the 'Hoode' family story. Many modern researchers have also 'fallen foul' of the tendency to name children with the same name as their father throughout Medieval times, and this may well be the case here, creating confusion as to the real date for the first original Robyn Hoode.

There is no reason to doubt that Robyn and Marian produced children and that at least one son, Robin (II), would not have followed his father into noble military service and lived to a similar age.

1217-1227: In 'Skelton's play (written before 1547) Marian, or Matilda, is finally poisoned in Dunmow priory by procurement of King John, as she has retreated to a monastic life in old age as was the custom of wealthy widows.

This would be poisoning by one of John's supporters continuing to act by royal appointment after John's death, unless both Robyn and Marian died before October in the year 1216? Either scenario is possible.

Little Dunmow Priory is an Augustinian (probably Templar) foundation dating back to around 1106 and is down in Essex – not that unusual a place for Marian to retreat to as the Northern Barons and the Earl's of Chester also held large areas of land and supported monastic foundations in the south of England, as did the Templars and Hospitallers.

It is immediately obvious that Skelton had unlimited access *by royal assent* to many earlier 'lost' works on Robyn Hoode that had survived the 400 years since the events they recorded, and all of which gave him a consistent and informed 'back-story' from which to write. He is probably the last person to use these 'authentic' sources before many were destroyed during the Dissolution Of The Monasteries and the English Civil War, corruptions then began to appear in the age of printing and with the invention of 'popular fiction' (which was an alien concept to earlier writers who felt they could only 'embellish facts' not change them completely).

1221: *The marriage of King Alexander II of Scotland takes place to Joan, daughter of King John Plantagenet, in York Minster.*

1220-1300: The title *'Robbing Hood'* starts to appear as a criminal 'nick-name' in records in the latter half of the 13th Century.

Various commonly quoted examples include:

Robert Hode – Tenant of the archbishopric of York, fled the jurisdiction of the King's justices at York in 1225, *Robert (de Kyme)* – Saxon robber, disturber of the peace and 'Earl of Huntingdon', outlawed 1226 then pardoned 1227, *Willam Robehod* – Robber in Berkshire 1261, *John Rabunhod* – Murder in Hampshire 1272, *Alexander Robehod* – Thief in Essex 1272, *Gilbert Robehod* – In Court in Sussex in 1286, *Robert Robehod* – Sheep Stealer in Hampshire 1294, etc.

In some cases the 'honorary title' developed into a family name, one of the earliest being *'Robynhod'* in the Sussex tax records of 1296, and *'Robert Hood'* a forester outlaw around Wakefield in the years 1316/17. his may indicate that the heroic legend had begun to take root and the name become 'respectable' even before the death of the original Robyn and his son, and exactly as the legends suggest.

1244: *Jerusalem is lost back to the Saracens and Turks.*

1248: *The 9th Crusade is followed by the 10th (1271), both failed, and Constantinople is recaptured by the Eastern Empire in 1261.*

1251: *The marriage of King Alexander III of Scotland takes place to Margaret, daughter of King Henry II in York Minster.*

1264-1272: Following directly on in the tradition set by the 'Robyn Hoode' family, between 1266 and 1272 Nottinghamshire, Derbyshire and Leicestershire were the center of a guerilla campaign led by 'Roger Godbeard' which ultimately required royal intervention.

Roger was a tenant of William de Ferrers, earl of Derby, in Swannington, Leicestershire, on the western bounds of the forest of Charnwood, and a member of the garrison of Nottingham

Derbyshire Moorland – Home To Roger Godbeard & His Men.

Castle in 1264. He supported Simon de Montfort in the Baron's War (1264-1265) but had gone into open rebellion by 1267 and threatened the safety of Nottingham. He was eventually captured by an old comrade from his Nottingham Castle days, Reginald de Grey of Codnot, in February 1272, imprisoned in Bridgnorth, then Chester where he was tried by Reginald before vanishing from the records - but not before the accusation is made that he was 'received and protected' by Richard Foliot (once Sheriff of Nottingham).

Royal letters concerning these incidents vividly record the state of affairs at this time:

"Through outlaws, robbers, thieves and malefactors, mounted and on foot ... wandering by day and night, so many and great homicides and robberies were done that no one with a small company could pass though those parts without being taken or killed or spoiled of his goods ... and no religious or other person could pass without being taken and

spoiled of his goods."

1271: *Marco Polo undertakes his famous 'travels' to Asia and China, bringing back to Europe the most amazing accounts of life far beyond the Middle East.*

The Reign Of King Edward I (1272-1307)

1272-1307: *Edward I ('Longshanks') Plantagenet takes the throne and ransacks the treasury of the London Temple to aid his fight against the Baron's Revolt. Eight years later Edward is attacked by an unknown assassin with a poisoned knife but his life is spared by the swift action of Thomas Bernard, then Master of the Knights Templar, who sends the right drugs to cure him.*

1280: The two characters 'Robin and Marian' figured in the French *"pastourelles"* and presided over the French May festivities of which *'Jeu de Robin et Marion'* C.1280 is a literary version.

In this tale Robyn and his companions have to rescue Marion from the clutches of a *"lustful knight"* and, chances are, this is just one of a number of Robyn Hoode tales spread far and wide across the Medieval map of a developing Europe – the question being did it travel from Northern England to France, or from France to Northern England? Have the French preserved popular Robyn Hoode stories from the 12th century now long lost to British audiences, or did their material migrate to the lands of the Northern Barons to 'infect' the growing legends of Robyn Hoode? While both are equally a possibility we will probably never know for sure.

1288: *The Ottoman Turks lay the foundations of Turkish power in Asia Minor eventually leading to:*

1291: *The entire Holy Land is finally lost to the Saracens & the*

Templars and Hospitallers are out of a job. Crusades, as such, come to an end, and the Knights Of St John Of Jerusalem eventually re-locate to the island of Rhodes in 1310.

1349: *The bubonic plague, or 'Black Death', reaches it's peak in Britain and Europe and changes the Medieval landscape Robyn would have known for ever.*

'Q' – 'Quelle' – The Original Story Manuscript Reconstructed

So what can we say concerning this 'legendary character' about which we apparently know nothing?

(Sir) Robyn Hoode I (Aumale) was born in the medieval village of Loxley in Staffordshire, on land owned by the Earls of Chester, in the winter of 1129, to Hawise (Countess) de Mortimer (Aumale) and her second husband who was a prominent forester possibly named Udard. Robyn already had four half sisters and three half brothers by Stephen de Aumale (who had recently died) and later had a younger sister by Udard who then also passed away leaving Hawise, by now in her late forties, to seek a third husband or to 'buy herself out' of the medieval marriage game. Robyn could not legitimately use the name 'Aumale' or 'Mortimer' so apparently chose the name of his distant ancestor through his mother's first noble marriage - Odo, Count of Champagne.

His mother then passed away and Robyn grew up surrounded by foresters and nobles, living for some 15 years as part of the household of Hugh de Kevelioc, Earl of Chester, his part relative, and some of the time at the moated manor house at Chartley no doubt assisting with the construction of the castle, until he reached 16 and could undertake military training for three years in Scarborough on lands owned by the Aumale family. Here he was also involved in castle construction and had his first taste of using his bow for profit and justice capturing a raiding Viking ship. The resulting 'booty' gave him the ability to construct his first chapel, some personal wealth, and a life-long vision.

Eventually Robyn encountered Little John and Will Scarlet (who turns out to be the son of his sister by the Earl of Macclesfield) and this 'team' of 'Youngermen' is given jurisdiction by the ruling 'conclave' of appointed 'lions' over forests at Barnesdale in Yorkshire, Sherwood in Nottinghamshire, and Plumpton Park and Ingleton in Cumberland, which all sit north of the river Trent and along strategic major medieval highways. At this point they may also have been given several permanent residences at Barnesdale 'shrogs', Blythe and Tickhill where Robyn entertained his 'guests' in South Yorkshire, Nottingham 'red cliffs', Stanage Edge in the Derbyshire, and a manor house belonging to the Earls in Leek Staffordshire.

Almost immediately the group attends a royal archery contest at Nottingham and Robyn ends up killing 15 troublesome foresters who serve William Pevril 'The Younger', Sheriff of Nottingham, and then get into a disagreement over Robyn and Will's land holdings with the wicked Abbot of St Mary's in York, robbing his baggage train.

At some point Robyn finds it necessary to travel down to London with John and Will where they also soon get involved in medieval politics and fight two Viking mercenaries led by a Turkish knight from the newly founded kingdom of Aragon in Spain in order to defend the honour of a Scottish princess who is then betrothed to Will. For some reason, however, they never get to marry.

We then find them back in Barnsdale where they encounter a dejected Templar 'Richard At The Lee' who has lost his son to prison and gone into debt to the Abbot of St Mary's Abbey in York trying to raise funds for his release. The outlaws steal the Abbot's money and give it to the knight who then goes to York and apparently 'repays' the crooked Abbot, gaining back his lands. Then Little John uses his skills to inspire the Sheriff of Nottingham to hold an archery contest where the outlaws are unfortunately recognized and flee to the castle of Richard at the Lee in Wrysedale who is then arrested. In escaping from the archery contest Little John is injured by an arrow in the knee and takes about a year to recover. Robyn then takes the fight back to William Pevril who is killed and his men defeated. It is now 1153 and Little John agrees to work in the employ of the new Sheriff of Nottingham for a year with the blessing of Robyn.

Archers named in the archery contest include William Scathelock who is a 'breaker of locks', Gilbert 'white hand', Little Much a miller's son, and 'good' Reynold. They are eventually joined by Little John's half-brother and Nottingham tanner Arthur-a-Bland, George-a-Green of Bradford and Wakefield who is a livestock compound keeper, and the castle cook from Nottingham. In another tale of this period 'Friar' or 'Father' Tuck (Sir Roger Tut of Tutbury) first appears as a fine bowman, along with the Scottish mercenary knight Guy of Gisbourne, who is a distant, hostile, and soon very dead relative of Robyn.

Other notable characters associated with Robyn's band include the potter of Barnsley, the nuns of Farnsfield who supplied napkins, shirts, and bands, Bateman of Kendal who supplied 'Kendal green' cloth, Sharpe of Leeds who supplied arrows, Jackson the bow maker of Rotherham, David of Doncaster, plus 70-110 plus archers.

Around the years 1154 to 1157 a pardon from the new King Henry II Plantagenet follows for Robyn and his men killing the corrupt Sheriff (or Sheriffs) of Nottingham, and Robyn builds a second chapel at Kirk Smeaton in Barnsdale.

At some point Robyn meets Matilda de Marmion (later Marian or Clorinda), a young daughter of the 'Marmion' family who hold Bagot's Park around Abbots Bromley near Chartley where the couple may have first met. She is younger than Robyn by as much as 20 years or more but evidently as good as any man. She can shoot a bow, ride, hunt, and fight, which one story has her doing for an hour when she first meets Robyn dressed as a page boy who he fails to recognize. Robyn asks her to join his band at which point she recognizes his voice from some earlier encounter and they settle down together.

Further adventures pit Robyn and his men against various new Sheriffs, monks, Abbots, knights, and foresters, and Robyn uses disguises such as a potter, monk, mercenary, even an old woman, to out-smart the authorities. There is even an entry in the 'Royal Court Rolls' for the "County Of Cumberland" which states that Robyn Hoode ('Holdelme') and his father Udard held Carlisle Castle under King Henry II successfully against the Scots for three months in 1173 when Robyn would be aged around 43.

Upon taking the throne in 1189 King Richard assigns the revenues of Derbyshire and Nottinghamshire to his brother John creating the traditional back-story for the tales of Robyn Hoode who is then thought to have helped Reuben of Stamford and his daughter escape the 'Massacre of the Jews' at York in 1190.

March to April 1194 and King Richard I is involved in a three day siege of Nottingham Castle. Robyn Hoode (now aged around 64) meets King Richard (his junior aged 36) in the surrounding forests. After a light hearted skirmish the two become friends saying farewell at 'Ye Olde Trip To Jerusalem' pub at the foot of Nottingham Castle walls. At this encounter Robyn is granted the right to marry Marian (a type of 'pledge' or 'betrothal') and given rights to her lands at Malaset in the Lancastrian Marches where he settles as a Squire and servant of the crown for the next 16 years up to 1210. Most of his younger followers then serve King Richard in his French wars, progressively die, or settle on Robyn's lands.

King Richard is killed in France and John crowned King in May 1199. John then tries successfully to rid himself of his virgin teenage Queen Isabella, Countess of Gloucester, who sends

Richard of Partington north for Robyn requesting that he come to London and champion her cause, which Robyn does. This really upsets King John who pursues Robyn north without success and is then made to uphold Robyn's earlier pardon upon his return to London. In the years that follow John confiscates English lands from Northern barons who take sides with Philip II of France.

It is likely that Robyn Hoode finally ends his period of 'courtly love' and marries Marian at some point between 1210 and 1213 under the great yew tree in the church yard at St Cuthbert's Church, Doveridge, thus legitimizing their children and combined property in the eyes of the church and the new ruling regime. It is highly possible that the couple already had a son (possibly two) and a daughter by this time. Robyn was about to retire as a knight and chose to become a hermit at Dale Abbey in Derbyshire, and Marian had intentions of becoming a nun.

Then in one final act of defiance in June 1215 Robyn Hoode, by now aged around 85, marched south under the banners of the Northern Barons to face King John and get him to sign Magna Carta. Not long after this John then sends 100 archers north to kill Robyn without success. The king follows six months later, loses his treasure in the Wash, and is then poisoned and dies at Newark in October 1216.

In the months and years that follow, the elderly Robyn has had enough, falls ill, and heads to a woodland church to be bled by a female cousin and her monastic staff. She allows treachery to be enacted upon Robyn by Roger de Roumare of Doncaster ('Red Roger') who is the youngest surviving inheritor of the Aumale family. Robyn kills him but dies in the arms of Little John requesting that he be buried "... at Wakefield, underneath the abbey wall." It is November 1217 and Robyn is now aged around 88.

He is buried under the supervision of the elderly Little John under the developing foundations of the Cathedral church of All Saints in Wakefield and our story ends with Marian being poisoned by a supporter of King John at Dunmow Priory, Essex, around the year 1216, Little John digging his own grave at Hathersage and being buried there not too long after this date, and Robyn's eldest son living into old age through the 13th century and continuing the family tradition of serving under royalty.

So, to sum up with the original stories in date order:

1129:   Robyn is born in the village of Locksley in Staffordshire.
1130 – 1145: He is raised and trained by the Earls of Chester while living at Chartley Castle and introduced to Little John as a young adult.
1146 – 1149: He is sent to garrison Whitby and Scarborough and do some 'fishing'.
1146 – 1149: **Robyn Hoode Goes Fishing.**
1146 – 1156: Then he is stationed principally in Barnsdale / Sherwood Forests along Great North Road.
1150:   **A Geste Of Robyn Hoode (Includes:) The Poor Knight / The Archery Contest / The Sheriff And Little John / Robyn Hoode And Guy Of Gisbourne.**
1156 – 1162: He builds up a strong fighting force of foresters, archers and knights. Most surviving stories are then set between 1150 and 1200.
1150 – 1162: **Robyn Hoode And The Potter.**
             Robyn Hoode And The Monk.
             Robyn Hoode And The Curtal Friar.
             Robyn Hoode And The Beggar / Shepherd.
1190:   Robyn saves Reuben from the 'Massacre of the Jews' at York.
1194:   Robyn meets King Richard at the siege of Nottingham Castle.

1193 – 1194: **A Geste Of Robyn Hoode (Includes:) Robyn Hoode And The King / Robyn Hoode And The Sheriff Of Nottingham.**

1210 – 1213: Robyn officially marries his 'betrothed' Marian at Doveridge and they already have two (or three) children and land at Plumpton Park.

1210 – 1213: **Robyn Hoode And Maid Marian.**

1215 – 1216: Northern Barons go to London for the signing of Magna Carta.

1217: Robyn Hoode the Hermit dies and is buried under the Abbey wall at Wakefield. Little John dies at Hathersage in the years following.

1217: **Robyn Hoode: His Death.**

1215 – 1295: Represents the life time of Robin Hood (Junior) and his sister.

By 1280 'Robin and Marion' start to appear in French May Festivals.

"God rest the soul of Robin Hood,
For a gentle thief was he,
As ever ranged the gay green wood;
God rest his company."

'An Adventure In Sherwood Forest' from Hone's "Year Book."

2

Who is (or Should be) The Original 'Robyn Hoode'?

What follows is a detective story to match any of the great mysteries of our own time. At a glance we can see all the evidence spread before us and, somewhere in this tangled web of Medieval Latin and anarchic intrigue, lie the biological threads of the real Robyn Hoode. Confusing as it is, persevere with this investigation and you will be rewarded.

In the ballad *'Robin Hood And The Stranger'* we are given vital information about Robyn when he first meets 'Will Scarlett'.

It is recorded that Robyn has a sister who's only son at this point is 'young Gamwell' (William Scathelock), born and bred in Maxfield (Macclesfield) and on the run for killing his father's steward, his father being the 'Earl Of Maxfield', from whom he was separated some time ago, possibly as a child.

This means that Robyn's sister was married to the 'Earl of Macclesfield' and produced a son called 'Gamwell'. Crucially it also means that the sister's father *is also regarded as Robyn's father* – literally or adopted.

The title *'Earl Of Macclesfield'* only came into being in 1679, however there was an 'Earl' over Macclesfield during the life of Robyn Hoode. Earl Ranulf III le Meschin of Chester (1120-1129) granted the town its first borough charter followed by Earl Ranulf IV de Gernon (1129-1153) and Earl Ranulf VI de Blunderville (1181-1232).

The crucial question in identifying all the characters in the original tale is: Which lady associated with these Earl's best fits

Robin's sister?

Hills And Moorlands Of The Macclesfield Forest.

Earl Ranulf III le Meschin of Chester (1120-1129): Is the 3rd husband of 'Lucy' who had already produced William de Roumare (Earl of Lincoln, born C1096) by her 2nd marriage to Roger FitzGerald (de Roumare), 1st Baron of Kendall and Lord of Bolingbroke.

She gave Ranulf III a son, Ranulf IV de Gernon (born 1099 and died 1153), and a daughter 'Alice' (who married Richard de Clare).

So what happens if Robyn's eldest sister was 'Lucy', wife of Ranulf III le Meschin?

Lucy (sometimes 'Lucy of Bollingbroke') was an Anglo-Norman heiress in central England probably related to the Saxon Earls of Mercia. Despite confusion she is now thought to be the daughter of Thorold, Sheriff of Lincoln, and her mother a daughter of William Malet (who died in 1071). She had inherited the 'Honour of Bollingbroke' from both the 'Lincoln' and 'Malet' families. She died C1138 probably too early in time to be Robyn's sister – even though this would explain why Robyn was believed by later researchers to be Anglo Saxon. This is NOT the family of the real Robyn Hoode.

What happens if William de Roumare (1), half brother of Ranulf II de Gernon, was the father (Earl) in the Will Scarlett story?

He marries Hawise de Reviers (daughter of Adeline Peverel) to produce daughters and a son William (Helie) de Roumare, who married Agnes de Aumale to produce William de Roumare (the last), who married twice but had no recorded children (hence 'the last'!) Assuming a normal life span of (say) 50+ years a generation it would be William (the last) who is perhaps the best candidate for William Scarlett.

The name 'Roumare' is probably compounded from 'Rouge-Mare' which, in Norman French, means 'Red-Pool' as in a 'blood-pool', 'blood-red', 'scarlet'.

In future legends the incredibly similar name William Scathelock or Scadlock (meaning 'lock-smasher') became confused resulting in two different characters, who may even be brothers, being confused into one.

In this instance Agnes de Aumale would therefore be Robyn's sister.

Agnes de Aumale was born C1115-1120 in Holderness in the North Riding of Yorkshire to Stephen de Aumale (1), Crusader on the 1st Crusade (born C1069 and came of age in 1090). and Hawise de Mortimer. They married before C1100 and had three legitimate sons – William, Ingelram, and Stephen (2), and 3 or 4 daughters, Matilda, Adelisa, (another possible daughter name unknown), and Agnes (the youngest).

Her father, Stephen de Aumale (1) was the Son of Odo, Count of Champagne, and Adelaide of Normandy (Countess of Aumale), sister of William The Conqueror.

Stephen (1) succeeded his mother as Count before 1089. In the conspiracy of 1095 against William II Rufus (King of England

1087-1100) the rebels wanted to place Stephen (1) on the throne as he was the first cousin of brothers William Rufus and Robert Curthose (Duke of Normandy). While Stephen was never tried for this attempt, his father Odo lost his English lands. Stephen was on the First Crusade under Robert Curthose and was eventually given back his father's lands in Holderness, Yorkshire, upon his return. He finally submitted to King Henry I in 1119. He married Hawise+ ('Countess') de Mortimer. Therefore Hawise+ de Mortimer's first marriage to Stephen (1) de Aumale made her the first real 'Hawise' (meaning 'Countess') de Aumale.

Stephen's life may account for some of the unsubstantiated and confused claims made of Robyn by later writers (e.g. dispossessed, lost lands, going on crusade, etc.) if Robyn was part of his direct family.

Hawise+ de Aumale then produced the three known sons and three (or four) known daughters already mentioned over about 18 years, and was around 47 when her 57 year old husband died about the year 1126, meaning she was too young to remain a single wealthy widow under the prevailing noble medieval traditions of the day. She was expected to marry again.

Enter a forester knight by the name of Udard (Odard) and the genuine entry contained in the *Royal Court Rolls* for the *County Of Cumberland* for May 1199 previously detailed. Udard is a knight who served the king during the unsuccessful Scottish siege of Carlisle Castle in 1173 and who is also mentioned in other medieval records for the years 1174-1179. If Udard could fight as a knight for the king at Carlisle Castle then he would have been born around the same time as Hawise+ de Mortimer (Aumale) and be the same age or younger. It can be deduced that Udard's son Rob (Robyn) de Holdelme (Hode / Ode) was also the right age in the Court Roll to have been born around the years 1129-1130.

Unfortunately no authoritive records have yet been

discovered to say exactly who Hawise+ de Mortimer (Aumale) married by name - but the facts appear to fit. Hawise+ married her second husband fairly soon after becoming single in 1126, gave birth to Robyn in 1129 after which it is thought Udard died leaving Hawise+ to consider a third marriage. The outcome is not known however she appears to have lived to a very great old age. Robyn was most probably her last child and 'Robyn's sister' (actually 'half sister') referred to in the Robyn legends is one of the previous four daughters, probably the youngest Agnes who was closest to Robyn in age.

The *'Garland'* tale *'Robin Hood's Birth, Breeding, Valour, And Marriage'* says that: *"His* (Robyn's) *mother was niece to the Coventry knight, Which Warwickshire men call Sir Guy;"* The same story goes on to say: *"His* (Robyn's) *brother was Gamwell, of Great Gamwell Hall; A noble housekeeper was he,"* probably referring to Robyn's older 'brother-in-law' (a concept as yet unknown in medieval times), or 'brother-in-arms', this being William de Roumare (2) husband of Agnes. This is further confirmed later in the tale where Robyn himself refers to Gamwell (Senior) as his *"dear Uncle"* - the husband of his sister.

We know that Robyn was quickly adopted into the household of Earl Ranulf II de Gernons, Earl of Chester, which implies Udard may have died quite soon after Robyn's birth. It is impossible to say exactly as the *"15 years"* Robyn then spends in Chester may have begun when he was already 1 and continued till he was almost 16 creating up to 24 months of variance. We also don't know the full details of why Hawise+ placed Robyn into adoption, although it may simply be for his training as a knight. Confusingly she is then followed by another 'Hawise' or Countess Aumale.

Agnes de Aumale: Daughter of Stephen (1) de Aumale and Hawise+ de Mortimer, married her first husband Adam I de Brus, Lord of Skelton (died 1142) and produced two children, William

Old Chester Castle Illustrated In 1727.

de Brus (died 1212), and Adam II de Brus, Lord of Skelton (died 1196).

This Adam I de Brus is thought to be the same Robert (1) de Brus, 1st Lord of Annandale (C1078-1138) in the line of the famous 'House of Bruce'. Robert (2) de Brus died around 1189 or 1194 and was buried at Gisborough Priory in the North Riding of Yorkshire. He was followed by William de Brus 3rd Lord of Annandale (died 1212) who obtained large estates in northern England from King John. He granted lands to the cannons of Gisburn and may be a good candidate for *'Guy of Gisburn'* the mercenary of the Robyn Hoode tales who clearly supports King John and is serving the King's Sheriff.

Agnes de Aumale then married her second husband, William de Roumare (son of William de Roumare, Earl of Lincoln, and half Brother to Ranulf II de Gernon, Earl of Chester,) producing 3 sons by him; William, Robert, and Roger, before his death in 1151. William (later Earl of Lincoln) was still a minor in 1165 so was born later than 1144. Agnes died after C1170, possibly at Skelton Castle in Cleveland, Yorkshire.

What if Robyn Hoode was the brother of Agnes de Aumale?

He would be either William, Ingelram, Stephen, or another 'illegitimate' or 'unrecorded' son of Stephen de Aumale or Hawise+ de Mortimer (probably of Hawise+ in later life).

William* de Aumale: Also known as 'Guillaume le Gros' (C.1101-1179) was born before C1109, of age in 1130, and married Cecily of Skipton. He died 20 August 1179 in Holderness, North Riding, Yorkshire, leaving a daughter Hawise (2) de Aumale (born C1160 in Holderness/died 1214 in Essex). He fought in the *'Battle Of The Standard'* in 1138 and was made Earl of Yorkshire, building the first timber castle at Scarborough. He was Count of Aumale (Earl of Albemarle), Earl of York, Lord of Holderness, and the eldest son of Stephen (Count of Aumale). This would neatly explain why Robyn Hoode was sent to Scarborough Castle for his military training.

Confusingly his daughter and heiress was another named 'Hawise' (Countess) of Aumale (died 11 March 1214) described by chronicler Richard of Devises as *"a woman who was almost a man, lacking nothing virile except the virile organs."* She married first William, Earl of Essex, who died in 1189, less than a year later she married secondly William de Forz of Olerton, commander of King Richard's crusading fleet (Richard traditionally being the match-maker). She produced a son and heir (William) then William de Forz died in 1195, so Richard gave her in marriage to third husband Baldwin de Bethune (Richard's companion in crusade and captivity) who died in 1212. King John proposed a fourth husband but Hawise declined and paid 5,000 marks for her inheritance, her dower lands, and *"that she be not distrained to marry"*. By 1213 she had paid just a thousand marks and died in 1214.

It is interesting to note that William Malet (2) (grandfather of

William* de Forz (le Gros / de Aumale)) married Maud Ferrers during the proposed lifetime of Robyn Hoode, uniting two families highly prominent in stories and locations surrounding the real Robyn Hoode.

Stephen de Aumale (2): Also known as 'Etienne le Gros' (C1112 & mentioned in 1150) was still living in 1150 and married the eldest daughter of Roger de Mortimer. They had a son William Crassus (le Gros) (died 1219) who became a noted kinsman and follower of the elder William Marshall (protector of the young King Henry III) placing the Aumale family right at the heart of the ruling elite.

Arms Of William Marshall.

Ingleram de Aumale: Also known as Ingelran / Enguerrand (mentioned 1150) died in France quite some time after 1115 and little more is currently known about him.

So, based on all of the above, we can now take a reasonable stab at a family tree for the real Robyn Hoode and his connected relatives:

3

Robyn's Immediate Family Tree Reconstructed

Father's Side

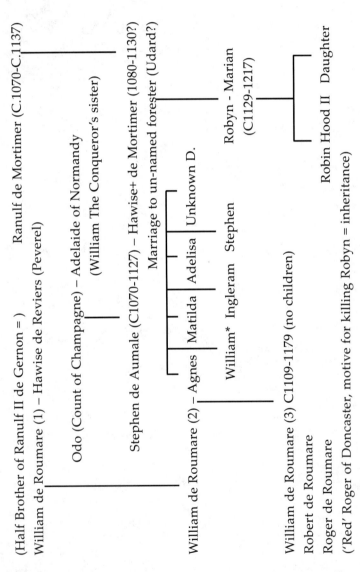

(Half Brother of Ranulf II de Gernon =)   Ranulf de Mortimer (C.1070-C.1137)
William de Roumare (1) – Hawise de Reviers (Peverel)

Odo (Count of Champagne) – Adelaide of Normandy
(William The Conqueror's sister)

Stephen de Aumale (C1070-1127) – Hawise+ de Mortimer (1080-1130?)
Marriage to un-named forester (Udard?)

William de Roumare (2) – Agnes   Matilda Adelisa Unknown D.   Robyn - Marian
(C1129-1217)

William* Ingleram Stephen

William de Roumare (3) C1109-1179 (no children)
Robert de Roumare
Roger de Roumare   Robin Hood II Daughter
('Red' Roger of Doncaster, motive for killing Robyn = inheritance)

If his 'kinswoman', the 'Abbess' at Kirklees Priory, was his 'cousin', i.e. an older lady two or more generations away from their common ancestor, who could she be?

The names 'Aumale' and 'Mortimer' are good candidates, a daughter of their 7 known children perhaps, but her intimate relationship with a 'Roumare' probably rules this family out (unless this was the original *'scandal'*?) Equally she may have been related in some way to Robyn's father (Udard / Odard) or a branch coming down from Odo, Count of Champagne, himself.

What about the mother's line as recorded by the various writers of ballads and tales?

Medieval Carving Of A Noblewoman's Head In Hathersage Church Yard Derbyshire.

4

Robyn's Family Tree in the Ballads

Mother's Side

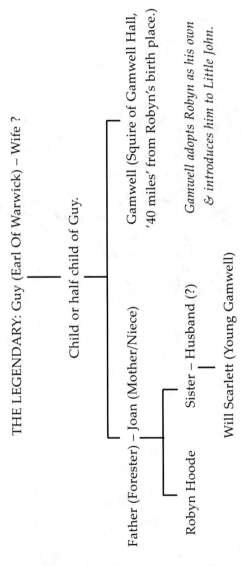

THE LEGENDARY: Guy (Earl Of Warwick) – Wife ?

Child or half child of Guy.

Gamwell (Squire of Gamwell Hall, '40 miles' from Robyn's birth place.)

Gamwell adopts Robyn as his own & introduces him to Little John.

Father (Forester) – Joan (Mother/Niece)

Sister – Husband (?)

Will Scarlett (Young Gamwell)

Robyn Hoode

In this reconstruction the Ballad Writers have used the legendary English hero of Romance, popular in England and France, 'Guy of Warwick' (Anglo-Norman 'Gui de Warewic') as the ultimate ancestor of Robyn Hoode's mother.

This is the character after whom the real William de Beauchamp, 9th Earl of Warwick, named his son Guy, 10th Earl of Warwick, in C1272. If there ever was a real 'Guy of Warwick' it is thought he probably lived in the late 10th Century / early 11th Century in the southern counties around Winchester.

This tree does not invalidate that of the Father's line as 'Joan' could be a proper first name, middle name, or 'nick-name' for Hawise+ (which isn't a name but a title meaning 'Countess'). Her line back to a legendary figure may have been created simply to fill a gap in the writer's knowledge, a gap now completed by the knowledge of the centuries, or to deliberately complete family connections between the Mortimers and Earls of Warwick.

The records we have examined through this section all need to be taken with a 'pinch of salt' as it was customary for wealthy patrons and religious establishments to re-write, doctor, or even 'invent' pedigrees, charters, land grants, and heroic stories to validate claims, or create a more romantic or prestigious lineage, sometimes even going all the way back to God! The material chosen here has been regarded with sensible suspicion in this respect and can never be regarded as more than a good set of guide-lines. Even the concept of 'personal names' was not fully established in the 11th and 12th centuries, and prominent figures frequently resorted to romantic or popular pet names and even to titles to which they were not entitled. It has been rightly called 'The Anarchy'.

5

Conclusions & Connections

Based on the above family connections, the intricacies and consistencies of Robyn's family in the legends, and the leading characters connected to the drama which is the life of the real Robyn Hoode, what can be said of the other major players often involved in these early tales? We can now establish some further significant support characters worthy of our attention.

Ranulf de Mortimer (Son of 'Guy') would be the child or half-child of the legendary 'Guy of Warwick' (who would therefore be his father) and, in reality, the Norman Baron Roger who actually assumed the name 'de Mortemer' from the area around his castle! The dates of Roger's life (born before 990, died after 1074) fit well with the legendary 'Guy' himself, or his immediate son, one of the ultimate ancestors of Robyn's mum in the legends and ballads.

Hawise+ de Mortimer / de Aumale / Countess of Albermarle (C1080-C1130 (?) / daughter with same name died C1189) is the daughter of Ralph de Mortimer and Melisande 'Millicent' de Ferrers, and mother of Robyn Hoode (referred to in the ballads by an apparent first name 'Joan'), born circa 1080 in the medieval city of Hereford, Herefordshire, England.

However Stephen de Aumale (C1070-1127) is NOT Robyn's biological father.

Stephen de Aumale was born about 1070 in Aumale, Seine-Inferieure, Normandy, France and died about 1127 in Holderness, North Riding, Yorkshire, England age about 57. Hawise+ was around 47 when her husband Stephen died and would certainly have been expected to marry again and to continue to produce children if she could. Evidently her next husband was a noble forester knight, possibly Udard (de Holdelme), by whom she had Robyn at some point in the years 1129 or 1130, probably the winter of 1129/30. Given Robyn's almost immediate adoption by the Earl's of Chester, Udard probably died after the year 1130, and it is Hawise+ daughter who lives till 1189. It is unrealistic to make the original Hawise+ 109 years old at her death but she must have survived to old age.

It would therefore be her daughter who was invited to marry by King John, but she declined and had to pay 5000 marks to get out of it (of which only 1000 marks were ever paid) and there is some evidence that she went on to become the first female 'Chief Forester of Sherwood' being described as in all ways male except in virility!

Her identity is confused by the existence of other ladies named 'Hawise' (which simply means 'Countess') alive at the same time, for example William le Gros' daughter born around 1160, was called Hawise 'Countess' Aumale, adding to a false impression of one individual having a very long life.

Stephen de Aumale and Robyn's mum Hawise+, daughter of Ralph de Mortimer of Wigmore, did produce an earlier son in the form of William le Gros (who died on the 20th August 1179) Count of Aumale (Earl of Albemarle), Earl of York, and Lord of Holderness. He was always going to be Hawise+ eldest first-born son and, therefore, the rightful heir to the family name 'Aumale' which is why Robyn could not legitimately hope to use this title.

Robyn Hoode / Holdelme / H'Ode / Odo (de Aumale) is the last and final surviving son of Hawise+ de Mortimer / de Aumale by a second husband, possibly named Udard (de Holdelme), when in her late 40's, born approximately three years after the death of her first husband Stephen de Aumale.

Further possible clues are found in 'Skelton's play for Henry VIII where Will Scarlett identifies a Friar to Robyn: *"He is of York;*

and of St Mary's cloister; There where your greedy uncle is lord prior." It would therefore appear that Robyn also had an uncle, his parent's brother or brother-in-law, who was Lord Prior of St Mary's Benedictine Abbey in York, probably between the years 1150 and 1220, and who often featured in the Ballads as Robyn's enemy. Clearly this relative viewed Robyn as an inferior addition to the family and may even be identified by name at some point in the future.

In 1132 a party of reform-minded monks left York to establish Fountains Abbey which may help explain the connections given to Robyn there in some tales from more recent times, and why relics relating to Robyn ended up there.

William de Aumale is Robyn's brother, half-brother, or 'adopted' brother (sharing the same mother), and married Maud Ferrers directly linking the Ferrers family into the Robyn legends and

Medieval Nobleman Hunting In The Forest.

allowing Robyn and his men to freely operate on Ferrers family land, exactly as they do in the legends. The Ferrers family also developed Tutbury Castle and Priory and most of the surrounding areas linking directly into Friar Tuck and ultimately Robyn's marriage at Doveridge Church.

Earl Ranulf IV de Gernon (1129-1153) was the son of Ranulf le Meschin and Lucy of Bollingbroke. At some time between 1135 and 1141 he married Maud (Matilda) FitzRobert of Gloucester (died 1189/90), daughter of Robert, 1st Earl of Gloucester, and illegitimate son of King Henry I. She apparently produced four children, Hugh de Kevelioc, Richard of Chester (d.1170/1175), Beatrice of Chester, and Ranulf of Chester.
While this is the very noble family into which Robyn was adopted, it does not fit the pattern of Robyn's own biological family. However:

Hugh de Kevelioc (1147-1181) married Bertrade de Montfort of Evreux (daughter of Simon de Montfort) and produced only one son, Ranulf VI, the rest daughters: Matilda de Blunderville (Matilda or Maud of Chester) who married David of Scotland (8th Earl of Huntingdon), Mabel, Agnes, Hawise, Beatrix, and possibly Amice. The name 'Kevelioc' is thought to be taken from his birth-place in Monmouth, Wales.

The lack of sons in the household of Earl Hugh may help to explain the adoption of Robyn, and the family link to David of Scotland may explain why later writers picked up on the 'Earl of Huntingdon' connection (especially with Robyn's various other later connections to Scotland and the Scots).

Agnes Of Chester, Daughter of Hugh de Kevelioc, married William de Ferrers (4th Earl of Derby) and they remained together for 55 years until it appears they both died in the same year 1247. They produced at least five children: William (de Fererrs – 5th Earl of Derby), Sybil, Sir Thomas of Chartley

Ferrers, Sir Hugh of Bugbrook Ferrers, and Petronile, creating direct family connections to the Ferrers family (as noted) and to Chartley Castle where Robyn probably spent his years growing up in the moated manor house there, and later while the castle was under construction.

Hugh de Kevelioc, Earl of Chester, is 'Gamwell' (Senior) and adopted Robyn into his household for 15 years as Robyn is Hugh's half-cousin through the line of Ranulf II de Gernon. Hugh died in Leek, Staffordshire, in 1181 and this is therefore possibly the best location to look for 'Gamwell Hall' which is, as the legend says, about 40 miles from both Chester and Nottingham at this location. In his 15th year Robyn went for military service to Whitby and Scarborough with William de Aumale (but somehow ended up as a fisherman catching French Vikings with his bow!).

Possibly 'Gamwell' is a northern nickname or corruption of the French family name 'Gernon', that of Hugh's biological father. As in the famous rhyme both Ranulf IV de Gernon and Ranulf VI de Blunderville, Chester Earls either side of Hugh, would be Robyn's *'Earl of Chester'* with whom he was associated in both life and legend.

Admittedly there are two strong candidates for 'Gamwell (Senior)', Hugh de Kevelioc (Earl Of Chester) in some legends and William de Roumare (2), who married Robyn's half sister Agnes, in other legends. This can be reconciled in the tales if 'Gamwell' is viewed as an affectionate title for Robyn's directly or indirectly related 'uncles', or may simply be a later writer's confusion of the title?

The Ferrers Family: Henry de Ferrers, became 1st Earl of Ferrers, Lord of Longueville, Normandy, and a Domesday Commissioner. He built Tutbury (or Titbury) Castle and Duffield Castle and was granted 210 manors and lordships throughout England and Wales by Duke William of Normandy for his conspicuous bravery and support at Hastings in 1066. 114 of these were in

Derbyshire and much of Nottinghamshire over which he held virtual rule. The family became the Earls of both Derby and Nottingham.

Henry's de Ferrers descendents are noted to have rebelled against King Henry II, taken part in the Crusades, rebelled against King Henry III, one family member was mistress to King John, another was poisoned, another was a notorious 'highway-woman', and one even has the infamy of being the only 'Peer of the Realm' to be hanged for murder!

The family, through its five hundred year gradual fall from grace, has held power over kings and has been crushed by them. Their titles have include; Earl of Derby (1190) and Nottingham, Sheriff of Lancaster (1223-1227), Baroness Berkely (C1300), Baron Chartley (C1271), Baroness Fitzwalter, Baron of Groby, and Baron of Oversley.

Was it a member of the Ferrers family who was 'Robin Hood' as some authorities claim? The answer is actually both yes and no!

The 1240s 'Robert de Locksley' was identified by antiquarians long ago. He was 'Robert de Ferrers' and it was actually the Loxley near Uttoxeter in Staffordshire which they owned and from which they took their name. This Robert had lands around Yelling in Huntingdon, however there is no mention anywhere of this man having the name 'Hood' or being called 'Robin Hood' and the time-period is clearly far too late for him to be the original. Despite the families rebellious reputation he also has no documented connection to outlawry in any authentic Medieval record entry found so far. He is a later victim of an existing name and reputation, and of owning the geographic area in which the real Robyn was most probably born and raised.

A 'Robert de Ferrers' does appear in a robbery entry from 1242 at a place called Jerdal in neighboring Northamptonshire and it may be the same 'Robert' or it may not. There persists a tradition in which one of the Ferrers was said to be 'Robin Hood' which could simply have come from this 1240s Robert de Locksley, but the connection to him as a name is a later invention not found in the original legends. Date-wise all these characters are also alive well after the original Robyn Hoode had died.

Earl Ranulf VI de Blunderville (1181-1232), eldest son of Hugh Kevelioc, was knighted in 1188/89 and married Constance of Brittany. Constance of Brittany was the widow of Henry II's son Geoffrey and mother of Arthur of Brittany with whom King John contested succession to the crown, clearly demonstrating the power of this family. Put simply, Ranulf VI de Blunderville, Earl of Chester, almost became step father to the king! However this marriage failed in 1199 and they both separated without children.

This is not therefore the family line of Will Scarlett and Robyn Hoode, however it is the powerful (indeed 'legendary') 'Ranulf' with whom Robyn was associated during his lifetime.

Ranulf VI was High Sheriff of Lancashire, Staffordshire, Shropshire (1216), Lord of Lancashire (1215), and witnessed the Magna Carta at Runnymede in 1215. He also fought for King John alongside William Marshall in 1217 defeating the French and their allies at Lincoln. He joined the Fifth Crusade (1220-1224), built the castles at Bolingbroke (Lincolnshire), Chartley (Staffordshire), and Beeston (Cheshire), founded Dieulacres Abbey (Leek), and died in 1232 leaving his estates to his four sisters. He is the 'Ranulf' about whom the famous ballad was written. He would also ultimately have been Robyn Hoode's superior commander.

Roger 'Hell' de Lacy (1170-1211) would probably be Robyn's military trainer as a knight and 'commander-in-chief'. The Earldom of Chester was virtually independent of the Crown during this time, and had its own Parliament of chosen Earls and Barons, and their tenants under the Earl. This is the structure into which Robyn Hoode fits as a servant 'yeoman' ('Youngerman')

De Lacy Tomb At Whalley Abbey.

knight under one of the independent ruling council of Chester, acting out their wishes, and ultimately those of Ranulf VI and King Richard I.

Study of the single 'Lion Rampant' found on the shields of the major players in the life of Robyn Hoode has revealed a new and hitherto unsuspected 'Order Of Knights' serving under King Richard I 'The Lion Heart' (1189-1199: **Red-Orange Shield / Black Lion**) or his ideals. Richard's 'Pride Of Lions' or 'The Lions Of The North', possibly a sub-division of the newly formed Knights Templar, consisted of himself plus:

William The Lion Of Scotland / House Of Canmore (1214-1249: **Red Shield / Yellow Lion**), Earl of Chester Ranulf I Meschin (1120-1129: **Yellow Shield / Red Lion**), Lady Dervorguilla Of Galloway & Cumbria / Daughter Of King David 1 & Matilda Of Chester (1210-1290: **White Shield / Red Lion**), Earl Ranulf II de Gernons (1129-1153: **Red Shield / White Lion**), Roger 'Hell' De Lacy (**Yellow Shield / Purple Lion**), Llywelyn The Great of Wales / Supporter of Northern Barons but married Joan daughter of King John in 1205 (1172-1240: **Yellow Border / Red Shield / Yellow Lion**), and William Marshall Earl of Pembroke /

Childhood Protector of King Henry III (**Shield Split Equally Yellow Left & Green Right / Red Lion**).

No doubt there were more 'Lions' but these are the surviving original shields for these knights used at the time and not their modern invented or 'retrospectively imposed' counterparts.

Sir (Father) Roger of Tutbury is 'Friar Tuck' ('Tut' or 'Tit') from the then recently constructed Ferrers family monastery at Tutbury. He appears in *'Robin Hood And The Knight'* and *'Robyn Hood And The Sheriff'* which both have written manuscript dates as early as 1475, making him firmly part of the original legends. He is not a later addition.

Further support for an early date comes from two royal writs dated 1417 which refer to Robert Stafford, a Sussex Chaplain who had assumed the alias of *'Frere Tuk'* who was evidently already famous far and wide well before this date. This Friar 'Robert' Tuck was still at large in 1429!

The real original 'Friar Tuck' would have been a second or third generation English Benedictine 'Black Friar', genuinely renowned in the brewing of wines and spirits, and initially resident at Tutbury Priory some time between the years (say) 1150 and 1210.

St. Mary's Priory Church, Tutbury, was probably founded on the site of an earlier Saxon church around the year 1086 by Henry de Ferrers and consecrated on the 15th August 1089, the festival of the 'Assumption of the Virgin Mary'. About 60 years later (around 1149) Robert de Ferrers built a Priory on the site staffed with 12 Benedictine brothers from the monastery of St Pierre-sur-Dives, Normandy, and the family continued to keep their foundation rich and powerful although, unusually, the Prior kept his affairs separate from the monks until 1230 when an agreement was drawn up for him to supply the monks foodstuffs in return for hospitality.

Oil Painting Of St. Mary's Priory Church Tutbury.

William Ferrers (Earl Of Derby 1190-1247) brought the body of his great grandfather Robert for burial at Tutbury and granted the monks many lands, the hermitage of Agardsley, and rights in Needwood Forest. It also appears that Tutbury Priory held forest at Doveridge which may explain the link between Marian (Maid Marmion) and Friar Tuck, especially if these characters were both English during a period that the French monastic estab-lishment was laying claim to local English lands!

Between 1100 and 1500 there were many disagreements between the French mother house and English monks as to who could appoint the Prior, regulations, tithes, etc. and this may even have contributed to Friar Tuck eventually leaving Tutbury Priory and becoming a somewhat 'independent minister' for an outlaw band.

Later in history, when the powerful Lancastrian lord John Of Gaunt married the only child of the first Duke Of Lancaster he made Tutbury Castle his home and the future king Henry IV spent his childhood there.

Matilda / Maid Marrion / Marian (Clorinda) is a lesser daughter of the Marmion family who owned lands around Chartley Castle, Abbots Bromley, and the Needwood Forest, the location where Robyn grew up (adopted by Earl Hugh) and where Ranulf VI then built his castle. They also owned lands at other locations in Yorkshire and the Midlands frequently associated with Robyn Hoode. Robyn may have first met Marian as a young girl between the years 1135 and 1150 while living at Chartley Castle or Loxley village, and later writers give the reason for a name change from 'Matilda' to 'Marian' so that Robyn can *'lawfully take her to wife'* as a *'spotless maiden'* in later life.

Presumably, up to this point, they had kept their relationship going as 'betrothed' under the conditions of Medieval 'courtly love' which basically allowed for the creation of children in youth while both parties could continue to pursue separate individual responsibilities to family and state – tied by oath and bond in chivalrous fashion but unmarried by the church. They have at least one son named 'Robin Hood' after his father, and a daughter.

Gamwell (Senior) is William de Roumare (2) who is married to Robyn's 'sister' (actually half-sister) Agnes. Agnes is the daughter of Stephen de Aumale (C1070-1127) and Hawise+ de Mortimer (1080-1129?) sharing the same mum as Robyn Hoode through Hawise+. This means that:

Will Scarlett is William de Roumare (3) (Will 'The Blood-Red') son of William de Roumare (2), he is often referred to as 'Gamwell' (Junior) and is probably around 15 years older than Robyn, being born around the year 1108, aged around 67 when they meet, and dead some time well after the accepted 1179 (say after 1189) but before Robyn retires to his lands at 'Malaset' in the

Lancastrian Marches.

Could this be the same *'William of Goldesborough'* (a village in Yorkshire) recorded as a name on the illustration of the supposed original grave slab of *'Robert Hood'*, along with the name *'Thomas...'* (Richard Grafton's *'Chronicle'* 1569)? We may never know.

In 'Skelton's play for Henry VIII the two characters Will Scarlett and William Scathelock say to their executioner 'Warman': *"Our mother saved thee from the gallows, Warman,"* and *"One mother had we both; and both our fathers to thee and to thy father were kind friends."* This implies that there may have been two 'Scarlett's and that 'Warman's father was a friend of the family. Is this the two eldest 'Roumare' brothers, William and Robert? This brings us to:

Roger de Roumare is 'Red' Roger of Doncaster, the youngest of the three legitimate heirs to the 'Roumare' house giving him a direct motive for killing Robyn in 1217. He is the younger brother of William de Roumare (3) who produced no children, and Robert de Roumare.

This complete family tree would give us: William de Roumare (3) Will Scarlett (or 'Gamwell' Senior?) son of Robyn's sister Agnes, Robert de Roumare, Will's brother William Scathelock ('Gamwell' Junior ?) also a son of Robyn's sister Agnes (which helps explain the later confusion of characters), and 'Red' Roger de Roumare of Doncaster, also a son of Robyn's sister Agnes and youngest legitimate heir to the family.

'Guy of Gisburn' is William de Brus, 3rd Lord of Annandale (died 1212), an avid supporter of King John, William is the real 'Guy of Gisburn', a Scottish knight or 'mercenary' and distant relative of Robyn through his sister's first marriage. He may well have been killed by Robyn at Barnsdale in 1212. This explains the great deal of Scottish interest in Robyn later in his life.

Little John or John Lytell (possibly 'Naylor') is a forester-knight living most of his known life in Hathersage, Derbyshire. 'Johanas Little', 'John Le Litel', 'John Little', and 'Littel John', are all also variant names associated with him. As for his birthplace, the *'Geste'* places this in Holderness, East Riding of Yorkshire / Humberside, and some authorities even suggest that he was the son of William de Faucumberg of Catfoss manor in Holderness, but we will probably never know for sure as he has not yet been found in any authenticated records or manuscripts of the time in the way that Robyn Hoode probably has.

The Cottage Of Little John Which Formerly Stood By The Church At Hathersage.

Robyn probably first meets John when Robyn is a young man aged 15-20 at the house of Hugh de Kevelioc (a 'Gamwell' senior) in Leek, Staffordshire, but we don't know how old John is except that he out-lives Robyn, implying that he is probably a bit younger. John dies at some point after 1217 and is traditionally buried in Hathersage where he was then living in a tiny cottage (now demolished) to the east of the church. It would therefore not be unreasonable to place John well into his 80's at death.

The celebrated English antiquary Elias Ashmole wrote in 1625:

"Little John lyes buried in Hathersage Churchyard within three miles from Castleton, near High Peake, with one stone set up at his head and another at his feete, but a large distance between them." *(Ashmole MS 1137:fol.147).*

According to legend he dug his own grave under an old yew tree in the graveyard, near to the old preaching cross, and directed that his cap, bow, and arrows should be hung in the church. A popular late Victorian poetic ballad adds:

"His bow was in the chancel hung
His last good bolt they drave
Down to the rocks, its measured length,
Westward fro' the grave.
And root and bud this shaft put forth,
When spring returned anon,
It grew a tree, and threw a shade,
Where slept staunch Little John."

Sadly these items disappeared from the church at some point in the 17th or 18th century, however a bow could be found at Cannon Hall, a seat of the Spencer family who were owners of Hathersage, and was always known by the name of *'Little John's Bow'*. It was of spliced yew and of great size (*"above six feet long"* though the ends where the horns were attached were broken off). It was displayed close to the brasses of the Eyre family who were appointed 'Hereditary Foresters of Peak Forest' which was a royal appointment, and for this service they were allowed a bovate of land at Hope between Hathersage and Castleton. Robert Eyre followed his father William in this position for which they received the high salary in those days of 12 pence a

day. They also held the official rank of *"Gentlemen Foresters"* which was a new rank of 'Itinerant Foresters' known as *"Bow Bearers"* (created by Edward I) who all carried a long bow as their sign of office, or the bow was borne by an attendant. It was a crown appointment carrying the very high remuneration for those days of a shilling a day and went to men of knightly rank.

In 1784 the local church vicar, Charles Spencer-Stanhope (died1874) wrote that the squires brother, William Shuttleworth

(who dug up John's body in the 18th century), hung a thigh bone reputedly from Little John's grave in his room. However, as it was thought to be bringing poor fortune to its owner, it was ordered to be reburied by his clerk but the clerk kept the labeled bone in his window as a curio. When the father of Charles Spencer-Stanhope (Walter Spencer-Stanhope of Cannon Hall and Horsforth Hall, 1749-1821) and Sir George Strickland were visiting Hathersage, Strickland is reported to have *"run away with it"* and it has not been seen since. Wherever it is, if it still survives, let's hope it retains its label!

It wasn't until around 1930 that 'Little John's Grave' was taken into the care of The Ancient Order Of Foresters and by 1935 the iron railings, the headstone, and the small stone at the side of the grave had been erected. The inscription on the headstone reads:

"Here lies Little John
the friend and lieutenant of Robin Hood.
He died in a cottage (now destroyed)
to the west of the churchyard."

6

Other Prominent Characters Associated with the Early Robyn Hoode

The House Of Plantagenet (Replacing the House Of Normandy)

King Henry II Plantagenet *'Fitzempress'* = Ruled: 1154-1189.
   Queen Eleanor of Aquitaine = C.1122-1204.
King Richard I Plantagenet *'The Lion Heart'* = Ruled: 1189-1199.
   Queen Berengaria of Navarre = C.1165-1230.
King John Plantagenet *'Lackland'* = Ruled: 1199-1216.
   Queen 1: Isabella Countess of Gloucester = Married 1189-1199 (Annulled).
   Queen 2: Isabella Countess of Angouleme = Married 1200-1216.
King Henry III Plantagenet = Ruled: 1216-1272.
   (Became King as a minor under the oversight of Sir William Marshall).
   Queen Eleanor of Provence = C.1223-1291.
King Edward I *'Hammer Of The Scots'* = Ruled: 1272-1307.
   Queen 1: Eleanor of Castile = Married 1254-1290 (Died).
   Queen 2: Margaret of France = Married 1299-1307.

The Kings Of Scotland (House Of Canmore)

King David I *'The Saint'* = 1124-1153.

  Queen Matilda Countess of Huntingdon = C.1074-1131.

King Malcolm IV *'The Maiden'** = 1153-1165

  (* maintained a life-vow of chastity and had no Queen).

King William 'The Lion' = 1165-1214.

  Queen Ermangarde de Beaumont = C.1170-1234.

Alexander II = 1214-1249.

  Queen 1: Joan of England = 1210-1238. (3rd child of King John Plantagenet. Died).

  Queen 2: Marie de Coucy = C.1218-1285.

Alexander III = 1249-1286.

  Queen 1: Margaret of England = 1240-1275. (2nd child of King Henry III. Died).

  Queen 2: Yolande de Dreux = 1263-1322.

The Earl's Of Chester

Earl Hugh I 'Lupus' (of Avranches) = 1071-1101 (Cousin of William 'The Conqueror').

    Married Ermentrude of Claremont.

Earl Ranulf I (Meschin) = 1120-1129.

    Married Lucy of Bolingbroke.

Earl Ranulf II (de Gernon) = 1129-1153.

    Married Maud of Gloucester.

Earl Hugh II (Kevelioc) = 1153-1181.

    Married Bertrade de Montfort of Evreux.

Earl Ranulf III (de Blunderville) of Chester = 1181-1232.

    Married Constance of Brittany (Annulled at her request).

This stormy arranged marriage produced Arthur I, Duke of Brittany, King Richard's own nominated successor, who is eventually imprisoned at Rouen Castle where he vanishes in April 1203 with King John being widely accused of having him killed.

    Married Clemence de Fougeres.

Earl John (the Scot) = 1232-1237 (Earl as the son of Matilda, sister of Ranulf III).

    Married Elen ferch Llywelyn (daughter of Llewelyn The Great).

The Sheriffs Of Nottingham During The Life-Time Of Robyn Hoode

William Pevril 'the younger' (poisoner) = 1129-1153.

(*Unknown Gap?* = 1153-1157).

Sir Robert Fitz Ranulf = 1157-1170.

William Fitz Ranulf = 1170-1174.

William de Ferrers = 1174-1177 +

(*Captured the castle against Richard de Lucy, Warden Of The Realm*).

Serlo de Giendara = 1177-1180 +

Ralph Murdac = 1180-1190 +

Roger de Lacy = 1190-1191 + (*For just 7 months then transferred to:*)

William de Wendenal = 1191-1194.

(*Who surrendered the castle to King Richard after the three day siege in 1194*).

William de Ferrers = 1194-1196 +

William Brewer = 1196-1200 +

Hugh Bardulf / William de Lech = 1200-1202.

Reginald de Karduil = 1202-1203.

(*Then followed almost yearly by various holders, sometimes several in one year*).

+ Once William de Ferrers captured Nottingham Castle from Richard de Lucy it appears it remained under the control of supporters of King Richard I until William de Wendenal took it seven months into the tenure of Roger de Lacy. Upon his return in 1194 King Richard simply marched to Nottingham and took it back!

Nottingham Castle As It May Have Appeared In The 12th Century Before Extensive Re-building In Stone.

7

Physical Evidence & Locations

Evidently the writers of Robyn Hoode legends were intimately familiar with the northern geography in which their tales were set. To name but a few prominent sites they included in the original legends:

Sherwood, Barnesdale, Nottingham, York, Staffordshire, Inglewood, Blythe, Tickhill, Bradford, Robin Hood's Bay, Wakefield, Derbyshire, Barnsley, Doveridge, Farnsfield, Deep-Dale, Kirklees, Plumpton Park, Newcastle, Scarborough, Lancaster, Yorkshire, Kendal, Leeds, Carlisle, Chester, Macclesfield, Hathersage, Wrysdale, Rotherham, Tutbury, Whitby, Loxley, Mansfield, even my own home town of Warrington, are all mentioned in the old legends.

Robyn attacks the train of the Bishop of Ely in Martin Parker's '*A True Tale Of Robin Hood*' killing and capturing 230 of the Bishop's men and the remaining 770 and the Bishop "*... set spurs to horse, and fled, To the town of Warrington.*" As a result:

> "*The Bishop, sore enraged, then,*
> *Did, in king Richard's name,*
> *Muster up a power of northern men,*
> *These outlaws bold to tame.*"

This quote and many others raise the question: Do any physical remains relating to the original Robyn Hoode, however obscure, still exist today that could warrant a visit? Surprisingly the answer is yes.

Despite the fact that the Georgians and Victorians re-named

Medieval Nottinghamshire In The 14th Century.

and invented hundreds of sites to associate with Robyn, there are some places that pre-date this relatively recent romantic obsession, some even contain archaeological evidence that may support their existence in the right time-period and at the right place for association with the real Robyn Hoode.

Some of these more important locations therefore demand a more detailed look.

In the one line place entries I have frequently attempted to give a map reference for the smaller, more obscure locations (the 'SK' number), and included a date (for example '= 1680') for the earliest surviving written reference to the place.

City Of Chester

The city of Chester contains a huge concentration of impressive archaeological and historic sites, most of which were standing in better condition than they are now back in the days of Robyn

Hoode. When William 'The Conqueror' rode into Chester in 1072 he would have seen most of the late Roman buildings still standing, a full circuit of Roman walls, and the Dark Age or 'early medieval' structures that had begun to spring up in the gaps. It is even thought that Vikings had established a manufacturing and trading base around the area of St Olaf's church facing the river Dee.

Earl Ranulf Le Meschin.

Looking specifically to things that would have been relevant to Robyn as he grew up there in his first 15 years, a good place to start would be St John's Church on the banks of the River Dee by the remains of the Roman Amphitheatre. There is a good display of Anglo Saxon and Viking stonework here produced by the 'Chester School' of stone masons, and an impressive collection of medieval tombstones covering the years of Robyn and the Earls Of Chester. A design to look out for is the distinctive '4 Torc Bracelets Forming A Cross' which was favoured by the Barons Of Halton and Earls Of Chester. These distinctive coffin lid designs can be found here in St John's, in Chester St Werburg's Cathedral, Norton Priory, Stanlow Abbey, Warrington Friary, and even as far afield as Bakewell Parish Church in Derbyshire.

A walk around the walls of Chester is also recommended as many sections of them are reconstructed or consolidated medieval walls. A visit to St Werburg's Cathedral is a must, and an investigation of the famous Chester 'rows' of two-storey shops, centering on the medieval town cross, will reveal hidden medieval features including an in-tact undercroft and 13th century pub.

Sadly most of the castle which Robyn would have known well is either more recent or closed to the public so a look at the outside is probably the best to hope for, however the medieval

Ranulf De Blunderville Earl Of Chester.

arches of the impressive Dee Bridge still stand, and St Olaf's church, up the hill from the bridge inside the walls, still denotes the centre of the 'Viking Quarter' which may have survived into Robyn's day when trade, leather manufacture and smithing took place there. Formerly Chester was a port directly attached to the Irish Sea but the harbour silted up at some point to become what is now the Dee racecourse – a disaster which may have happened close to the times of Robyn Hoode.

It is also worthy of note that wherever the Earls Of Chester had significant land holdings they also established villages by the name of 'Loxley'. Chester itself was no exception – recent investigation has revealed that the area just across the medieval Dee bridge was probably referred to as one of these 'Loxley' villages.

Chartley Castle Ruins, Loxley & Abbots Bromley

Chartley Castle is the closest administrative seat to the Staffordshire village of 'Loxley' where Robyn is said by the early antiquarians to have been born and lived, and is one of the virtually unknown castles built by the Earls Of Chester.

In the landscape behind the current impressive ruins lie an Anglo Saxon / Norman moated site with associated bailey settlement features, and a supposed

Roman fortification enclosure. It's not the castle but the square moated site which is almost certainly the residence to which Robyn would have moved locally during the 15 years he was with the Earls Of Chester. The castle was still in the planning stage with construction only commencing in Robyn's senior years.

Robyn is born at Loxley, lives at Chartley, first meets Marian from Abbott's Bromley on her families Bagot's Park estates, marries her at Doveridge, and has countless connections to Tutbury, all of which are within a day's walk of each other. Nowhere else in the geography of Robyn's life do so many historically authentic and prominent locations come together in such a consistent and convincing way. It is therefore doubtful that anywhere else could place as good a claim to being the original source of the real Robyn Hoode.

One thing which becomes obvious to any researcher early on is that Robyn's land holdings seem to correspond well to those of the Earls Of Chester, indicating the noble military and family links here early on. As has already been noted the same place name 'Loxley' also appears amoung the Earl's lands in Staffordshire, Warwickshire, Derbyshire, and Yorkshire, which has created much confusion with researchers down the years. For example the Earls Of Chester have holdings at: *Chartley Castle / Tutbury / Robin Hood's Bay / Pillerton Priory / Pevril Castle* (by marriage), Robyn Hoode (frequently styled 'Robin Of Loxley - Earl of Huntingdon' also appears to have holdings at: *Loxley Staffordshire / Robin Hood's Bay / Loxley Warwickshire / Loxley Chase and Loxley west of Sheffield / and the Peak District.*

The magnificent surviving forester's tradition that is 'Abbott's Bromley Horn Dance' is notable in that it includes 'Maid Marian' but significantly leaves Robyn Hoode out, having instead just 'an archer', which may be a clue that this was the Marian / Marmion family estate and not that of Robyn. The first mention of Abbotts Bromley appears in 942 when it is named *'Bromleige'* and is given to the Saxon 'Wulsige the Black'. It stays in Saxon hands until it passes to Wulfric Spot, Earl of Mercia, who wills it in 1002 to the Abbey of Burton. Here it is recorded as a village with a large woodland and probably a church ("*a priest*") in 1086. As an ecclesiastical village with no 'Lord Of The Manor' it prospered and had a regular market by 1227 when this was confirmed by Royal Charter. By this time the Abbotts Bromley Horns were already in existence in some form having now been carbon dated back to around 1065 by the Department Of Geological Sciences at Birmingham University, making them already a couple of generations old by the time Robyn was born.

The Magnificent And Mysterious Ruins Of Chartley Castle Staffordshire.

St Nicholas Church & The Bagot's Park Estate

In a side chapel of the Church of St Nicholas in Abbot's Bromley Staffordshire is a collection of deer horns mounted on wooden heads suspended from brackets on the walls. These are carried into the market place on a day known locally as 'Wakes Monday' and there the famous 'Horn Dance' is performed by a team of twelve dancers and attendants, not unlike Morris Dancers in appearance, around the same time every year.

Six of the dancers use the horns and there is a Hobby Horse, a

**Waiting For The Horn Dancers Outside The Crown Pub By The
Village Green In Abbot's Bromley.**

'Fool in Motley', a boy with a triangle, another with a bow, the
'Maid Marian', and an accompanying musician. Marian carries a
long-handled ladle (or more recently a bucket) for collecting
contributions from appreciative spectators and the whole troop
first perform to the village, then march out to farms and the
larger houses, returning later in the day to conclude in the local
inn where the traditional toast is *"The Horn Dance of Abbot's
Bromley, long may it continue."* As already mentioned, the notable
absence of Robyn Hoode but the presence of Marian effectively
'collecting tithes' speaks volumes for the medieval aspects of this
ritual set against the surrounding lands and forests owned by the
Marmion family.

Some historians say the ritual commemorates the granting of hunting privileges in Needwood Forest during Norman times when forest laws were exceedingly severe, others maintain the dance was held to celebrate the chase, and still others project the ritual use of stag horns and dancing back into prehistoric times, linking the ritual with the stag antler head pieces found at Starr Carr (Yorkshire) and other prehistoric sites around Europe.

If you want to visit the village to watch the Horn Dance it is performed annually on the first Monday following the first Sunday after the 4th of September and is well worth a visit. Village festivities usually last all day.

Doveridge Village & St Cuthbert's Church

It is said that Robin married Marian under the great yew tree in the church yard at St Cuthbert's Church, Doveridge, and this tree has been authentically established as being around 1600 years old making it at least 500 years old at the time of Robyn. This illus-

trates well the approach taken to many of the sites associated with Robyn as some fail this 'age test' for example Sherwood's 'Great Oak' was only an acorn sprout when Robyn supposedly hid in it!)

The Doveridge Church story goes like this:

"Said Robin Hood, lady fair,
whither away,
Oh, wither fair lady away ?
And she made him answer, to kill a fair buck,
For tomorrow is Titbury day."

"When dinner was ended
Sir Roger the parson of Dubbidge
Was sent for in haste;
He brought his mass book, and
He bade them take hands,
And he joined them in marriage
full fast."

(Roxburgh Collection, British Museum, London. Original language thought to indicate a 14th Century date for composition).

This site is well worth a visit as the yew tree has been well preserved and supported over the years, and much of the fabric of the church, its churchyard cross, and its general surroundings date back to medieval times.

Tutbury Castle & St Mary's Church

Tutbury is a key site much overlooked by many Robyn Hoode investigators, especially those who reject 'Friar Tuck (Tut)' as a late invention (which he clearly is not).

The town was the main hub of activity for the area in medieval times and was extensively developed by the prominent Ferrers family who appear to have sheltered Robyn and his men on their lands and appointed the famous Friar Tuck to their religious foundation. While most of the castle ruins are of a later date, they are open to the public at set times, the medieval Priory Church of

Early Painting Of The Interior Of Tutbury Castle.

St Mary's is well worth a visit with it's imposing 11th century west front, and the charming town still retains much of its basic rambling medieval layout.

In the castle café there is a carving of a 'grimacing demon' figure which has the feet of two legs sticking out from below his arms. He was discovered in the castle moat and is believed to date back to prehistoric times and to represent a 'Celtic Demon' dragging a poor dead soul off to the 'other-world'. Maybe Robyn himself was also familiar with this distinctive grotesque carving displayed on the outside of the castle walls.

The Forest Of Barnsdale & Wentbridge

A popular misconception is that Robyn only operated in Sherwood Forest as we have it today. Back in the 12th Century the forest stretched all along both sides of The Great North Road (A1/M), the Roman Watling Street, and Robyn clearly moved north and south along this boundary as circumstances dictated. The huge area

ROBIN HOOD - WENTBRIDGE.
One of the only place names that can be located in 'A Lytell Geste of Robyn Hode' (c.1492-1534) is the Sayles now known as Brockadale. Wentbridge.
'And walke up to Saylis,
And so to Watlinge Stret (e),
And Wayte after some unkuth gest,
Up Chance ye may them mete.'

of the Forest Of Barnsdale once lay between Doncaster and Ferrybridge in South Yorkshire, 15 miles north of Nottingham, and still survives in the name 'Barnsdale Bar'. The place name 'Sayles' (Saylis) is also mentioned in Robyn Hoode tales, along the Great North Road / Watling Street where Little John could stand and look down *into Barnsdale*.

All these sites come together around the modern village of

Wentbridge, four miles south of Pontefract, where it is thought Robyn extracted payment for passage in the *'Ballad Of Robin Hood And The Potter'* and that he had his camp in the nearby Went Valley. The village bridge has the only official 'Blue Plaque' dedicated to Robyn Hoode, granted based on locations given in the various original 15th century *'Geste'* tales.

However, the best candidate by far for the chapel Robyn built in stone *'in Barnsdale'* is St Peter's Church at Kirk Smeaton (the neighbouring village to Wentbridge) which was recorded as

being there in the Domesday Survey in 1086 and still contains 12th and 13th century stonework and coffin lids in the fabric of the building. The archaeological evidence points to this as Robyn's second stone built chapel and the one featured in all the outlaw tales.

The other boundary down which Robyn moved was the north side of the River Trent, heading south from Barnsdale and Sherwood and we will return to these areas later.

Lee in Wrysdale

This is the hamlet thought most likely to be the legendary home of the knight *'Richard at the Lee'* whom Robyn befriends in the original *'Geste'* story where the place is given as *'Uterysdale'* (Wrysdale). The precise location of Richard's double-ditched motte and bailey castle is yet to be established but would certainly stand out as a distinctive medieval feature in the environment.

Scarborough, Whitby, & Robin Hood's Bay

Scarborough Castle contains evidence for Bronze Age, Iron Age, Roman, and Saxon development, with evidence on the Roman Station site for a Saxon Chapel thought to have been destroyed during the invasion of Harald Hadrada in 1066. This 'travesty' may have been the inspiration for Robyn Hoode building a better chapel in 1149 when his family ('Aumale') was actively taking an interest in developing the area.

Before 1500 Robin Hood's Bay was a more important port than Whitby and possessed Old St Stephen's Church on the hillside at Raw above the present village and which replaced a 'Saxon' church there (finally demolished in 1821).  This is most likely to be the chapel on *'Whitby Strand'* referred to in the story *'Robin Hood's Fishing'*, which Robyn would have effectively re-built in stone from the original decaying Saxon timber structure as his first venture into chapel building. This public spirited act also moved the principle chapel for the area away from the private military castle which was then under construction and further away from the coast with the risk of attack.

Huddersfield

While now a modern sprawling town, Huddersfield was recorded as 'Oderesfelt' and 'Odresfeld' ('Odo's Field') in the Domesday Survey of 1086. There has been a settlement in the area for over 4000 years, with a Roman fort being unearthed at Slack near Outlane, west of the modern town, and the prominent Castle Hill was the site of an Iron Age hill fort.

The original place name speaks of a family in the area with a very early Saxon, Norse, or Norman name that may relate to 'Hode', 'Odo', or even 'Holdelme'. Possibly the original Robyn Hoode family held lands, or continued to hold lands over time, somewhere here at this location.

Robin Hood's Well - Yorkshire

The present Georgian stone canopied structure was designed by the playwright architect Vanbrugh in the early 18th Century but the well is recorded here in the 15th Century, along with 'Robin Hood's Stone' (now on the opposite side of the motorway) used as a boundary marker by the monks of Monkbretton, Bansley, in a land related document of 1422.

The current structure stands at Skellow on the east side of the southbound carriageway of the A1, just south of Barnsdale Bar, but it has been moved from its original location against a field boundary wall when the A1 was constructed as a modern highway now sadly making it just an empty restored folly.

The actual well Robyn would have known on his travels lies opposite it, under the carriageway! It was the only physical site known anywhere to have direct documented historic name associations with Robyn at a date as early as the start of the 15th century and it is now essentially gone.

Nottingham Town

In *'Robin Hood And The Monk'*, Robin visits mass at St Mary's church in Nottingham where he is spotted and betrayed by a monk but then avoids capture by the Sheriff, which he does again in *'Robin Hood And The Potter'*. Many of the tales include visits to Nottingham and the surrounding areas where there are various hangings, rescues, deceptions, episodes in markets and pubs, encounters with the various Sheriffs and their wives, and quite a few battles and deaths. Clearly Nottingham is central to the later part of the life of Robyn Hoode.

Worthy of visiting today is the almost completely re-built castle which hides a fascinating warren of much earlier tunnels, underground store chambers, and the world's oldest flushing in-

Nottingham Castle Medieval Gates C.1890 Before Rebuilding Work.

door medieval toilet! Of the above ground castle structures only the lower part of the gate towers and the gate arch itself would be familiar to King Richard and to Robyn, the rest of the two gate towers are 20th century rebuilds.

The famous Robin Hood bronze statues and story plaques are just outside the castle (in the dry moat area to the left of the main gate), as is 'Ye Olde Trip To Jerusalem' pub, further round the castle rock to the left, where Robyn traditionally said goodbye to King Richard after the siege of 1194. The pub is partly set into the medieval cave system which formed the castle brew-house lending an element of probable reality to the story – but watch out for the dusty and cursed 'haunted galleon' which must never be cleaned!

The only other location with possible Robyn Hoode associations (now long forgotten) was:

Robin Hood Close – Nottingham (SK Unknown) = *'Robynhood Closse'* in 1485.

Robin Hood's Well - Nottinghamshire

Distinguished 18th Century travelers were treated to Robin's supposed chair, bow, and slippers at this location, which is mentioned in documents dating back to 1500.

In 1797 John Throsby recounts in The Antiquities Of Nottinghamshire: *"At the house we were formally shown several things said to have belonged to Robin Hood; but they are frittered down to what are now called his cap or helmet and part of his chair. As these things have passed current for many years, and perhaps ages, as things once belonging to that renowned robber, I sketched them."*

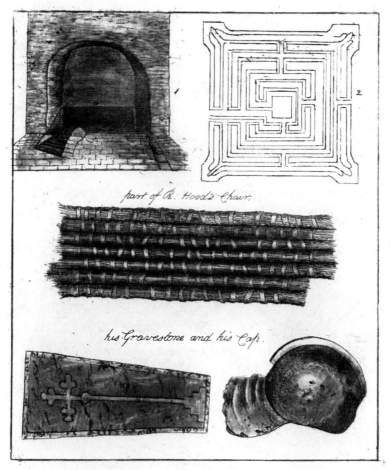

part of R. Hood's Chair.

his Gravestone and his Cap.

Robin Hood obiit xxiv kal Decembris mccxxxvii

This is, in fact, St Anne's Well, to the north of the town of Nottingham, set within the bounds of Sherwood, where there was a house, bowling green, and pleasure ground up to 1800, and a well under an arched stone roof of which water John Thorsby also wrote *"it will kill a toad"*. This is where a chair and a cap (or helmet) were kept that once belonged to Robyn Hoode.

These relics may later have moved to the well in the grounds of Fountains Abbey which claimed Robyn's Tombstone, 'Cap',

Chair, Bow, Arrow and Slipper right up to the start of the 19th century.

Robin Hood's Well – Nottingham (SK 589419) = *Robynhode Well* 1500.

St Anne's Well – Nottingham (SK 589419) = *Seynt Anne Well* 1551.

Fountains Abbey Yorkshire

Despite the fact that Fountains Abbey was founded by monks from St Mary's in York (often referenced in early Robyn legends), Fountains Abbey appears in connection with Robyn Hoode only in very late versions of legends developed after the 17th century.

In the 18th century 'Robin Hood's Well' at Fountains Abbey (which still stands) was the last place to display physical relics belonging to Robyn Hoode including his Tombstone, 'Cap' (helmet), Chair (or fragment of a chair), Bow, Arrow and 'Slipper'. These relics were there up to around 1800 but no one seems to know where they are today and the 'trail' leading to finding them is now over 200 years 'cold'!

Derbyshire & The Peak District

Pevril Castle, Castleton, was always the main power base in the Derwent Valley area and stands over the town of Castleton as a fine ruin which can still be visited by a steep climb. This was the home of William Pevril 'The Poisoner', apparent enemy of the Earls Of Chester, and someone clearly out of favour with the crown.

This whole area is replete with sites associated with Robyn Hoode, although many are only recorded in later times when the legends had a resurgence of popularity, some sites may ultimately prove to be genuine. Sites in the wider area include:

The Ruins Of Pevril Castle Lie In The Trees On The Hillside Centre Right.

Robin Hood's Bower – Greno Wood, Sheffield (SK 332945) = 1637.

Robin Hood Hamlet & Inn – Near Baslow (SK 280721) = *Robin Head* 1842.

Robin Hood Hamlet – Near Whatstandwell (SK 332551).

Robin Hood Inn – Lidgate West Of Holmesfield (SK 308778) = 1820.

Robin Hood Inn – Stannington Near Loxley, Sheffield (SK 307891).

Robin Hood Moss – Howden Moors (SK 190930).

Robin Hood's Picking Rods – Rowarth (SK 006909) = 1842.

Robin Hood's Spring – Howden Moors (SK 193933).

Robin Hood's Stoop – Ancient boundary stone Offerton Moor (SK 217807).

Robin Hood's Stride – Harthill Moor (SK 223623) = *Robin Hood's Strides* 1790.

The 'Stride' is a stand-alone distinctive rock feature on Harthill Moor by Youlgreave, which has other significant surrounding

details that include the remains of a prehistoric stone circle (once having nine stones, now just three), a sunken Medieval track way, and a forest chapel (Hermit's Cave) in the woods to the west which has an early medieval carved crucifix and niche where an altar would have stood. Here there are also two ancient yew trees, probably at least medieval in age, and evidence for the hermits cell roof-line carved into the rock face.

The 'Stride' itself would have been a fine outlaw's lookout post and the 'forest chapel' would have served folks during the time in King John's reign that churches and religious institutions were closed and allowed private worship in times of persecution.

Robin Hood's Table – Barbrook Valley (SK 277755) = Pre 1860.

Robin Hood's Tree – Wharncliffe Crags (SK Unknown) = No Longer in Existence.

Robin Hood's Well – Longshaw Estate (SK 267799) = 1809.

Robin Hood Well – Low Hall Wood, Sheffield (SK 333965) = 1773.

Robin Hood's Well – Monk Wood, South of Dronfield (SK 349764).

Robin Hood's Cross – Bradwell Edge,

Loxley Valley – West of Sheffield,

Robin Hood's Cave – Stanage Edge (SK 244836).

Robin Hood's Cave lies half way up the cliff which is the 'Stanage Edge' geological escarpment feature which formed the Medieval

boundary between Derbyshire and Yorkshire, effectively taking the cave out of the jurisdiction of both counties (a perfect hiding place for an outlaw), and close by in the valley below is 'Hood Brook'.

Chatsworth House

Robin Hood's Leap – Chatsworth Park Estate = Pre 1790.
Robin Hood's Stone – Chatsworth Park Estate = Pre 1790.

By mid Victorian times (C1840) a story was generally circulating called *'Robin Hood's Leap'* that was described as stretching back *"beyond living memory"* and concerned the wide chasm and nearby stone at the back of the Duke of Devonshire's grounds at Chatsworth Derbyshire.

In the story Robin escapes the Sheriff's men in Nottingham and comes to Edenshore on the Derwent where he meets the beautiful Kitty Ray, they fall in love, but Robin is forced to flee again. When it's safe she goes out to meet him and he returns, leaps across the wide chasm into the arms of his beloved Kitty, and they live together for the next two months.

Statue Of Pan In Chatsworth Woods.

How this fits into Robyn's life and what happens next is anyone's guess! Presumably the relationship doesn't last and they part for reason or reasons unknown? Given the overriding guide lines of chivalry and 'courtly love', it is hoped that this story fits the time in his outlaw years when Robyn and Marian are apart without any immediate hope of ever being reunited, maybe in the 1150s, and certainly before he meets her again and his official 'betrothal' by King Richard in 1194!

St Michael's & All Angels Church, Hathersage

Little John's Grave – Hathersage Church Yard (SK 231815) = 1680.
Little John's Cottage (Demolished) – Just East of Hathersage Church (SK 231815).
Little John's Well – Longshaw Estate (SK 267794).
Hood Brook – Hathersage (SK 230835).

This is the traditional resting place of Little John and the church currently has a medieval forester's tombstone in the front porch, just to the right as you enter, which has had the later letters 'L' and 'J' carved into it – possibly in the 18th century judging by the letter type. The church yard hosts the impressive site of 'Little John's Grave', and Little John's tiny stone-built cottage stood nearby into early Victorian times (but now sadly demolished).

The View From Hathersage Church Yard - Last Resting Place Of Little John.

The reputed 'Bow Of Little John' hung on the Wall of Hathersage Church until 1729. From here it was taken by the Spencer-Stanhope family to Cannon Hall in Cawthorne where it was observed in the early 1950s to be a recurved thick heavy bow, one end broken and the other tipped with a horn, hung below the minstrel's gallery in The Ballroom. Its current location is

unknown.

This bow apparently looked nothing like the one shown in a photo taken at Cannon Hall during the inter-war period showing *Little John's Bow*' held by archaeologist H.C. Haldane of Clarke Hall near Wakefield. This bow actually looks similar to one still housed in the Cawthorne Museum today.

Two other bows of similar type and age were recovered by workmen from rafters during demolition of a medieval timber framed 'cruck' barn at a farm somewhere in South Yorkshire during the 1980s but recording of more precise details, including location, was not done at the time and the bows were eventually recovered from the finder at a car boot sale without any further details being available. If nothing else however this does show that significant finds could still be made in relevant areas, and that small numbers of the millions of medieval long bows which must once have existed have survived.

Two Medieval English Yew Long Bows Found In A South Yorkshire Barn.

Sherwood Forest

Of the original royal medieval hunting forest of Sherwood only about 450 acres remain, even allowing for the fact that 'forest' did not mean entirely wooded back in the days of Robyn and his men. Furthermore it is difficult to tell where one 'forest' ends and another begins! Virtually all the forests recorded north of the river Trent tend to link up to form a long, sweeping, 'green barrier' that eventually heads north into Yorkshire. However many interesting sites of note do still exist:

The Green Wood - Sherwood Forest Nottinghamshire.

Robin Hood's Cave – Near Annesley, Sherwood (SK 510544) = 1700.

This collection of artificial caves in the rocks just outside the village of Rainworth are said to have been one of Robin's outlaw camps and this is certainly possible if they date back to occupation by the Ancient Britons before the Roman invasion as popularly thought.

Robin Hood's Chair – Robin Hood Hills, Sherwood (SK 516546).

Robin Hood's Cross – Pleasley (SK 504642).

Robin Hood Farm – Near Calverton, Sherwood (SK 582494) = 1840.

Robin Hood Hill & Pit – Near Oxton, Sherwood (SK 635538) = 1825.

Robin Hood's Hills – Near Annesley, Sherwood (SK 5615547) = 1775.

Robin Hood's Larder – Was a large tree in Sherwood Forest (SK 697676) where Robin Hood was said to have hung his venison. It survived into the late 1950s at which point it finally ended its life and collapsed.

The current 'Great Oak' is another large tree in Sherwood Forest located not too far from the Visitor Centre. This tree is evidently a fake as it would have been nothing but a tiny acorn sprout at the time Robyn was alive and not something he could hide inside! Current opinion favours it possibly being grown from an acorn off the actual medieval tree, which may have already been hundreds of years old in the days of Robyn Hoode – but, in reality, who knows?

Robin Hood's Stone – Near Newstead Abbey, Sherwood (SK 544541).

Robin Hood's Piss Pot – Near Blidworth, Sherwood (SK 610536).

Robin Hood's Well – Near Beauvale Priory, Sherwood (SK

497491).

Robin Hood's Cave – Creswell Crags (SK 535743).

Robin Hood's Grave – Near Creswell Crags (SK 540730) = *Robins Grave* 1840.

Robin Hood's Chair – Hope Dale (SK 213820) = 1882.

Robin Hood's Croft – Above Ladybower Reservoir, Lead Hill (SK 197867).

Robin Hood Cross – Bradwell Edge (SK 183803) = *Robin Crosse* 1319.

Robin Hood's Whetstone – Near Clipstone (SK 604623).

PAPPLEWICK and NEWSTEDE.

These places are not distinctly related by Thoroton. In what may by denominated the former is the domain of the honourable Frederick Montague. The village here is pleasantly situated, near the delightful pleasure grounds of that gentleman. Here are extensive cotton-mills which employ many hands.

In this lordship is a hollow rock called Robin Hood's Stable, handed down, as such by tradition; it is a curious Cave on the side of a little hill, on a farm, of Mr. Montague's, near the Lodge at Papplewick-Hall. Hayman Rook, Esq. who favoured me with the drawings of the entrance and internal appearances of this Cave, from which the views below are taken, thinks there is a great probability of its being used by that celebrated depredator.

No. 1, is a perspective view of the entrance before the present door was put up and the wall erected.

No. 2, is a view of the inside. This Cave evidently appears to have been cut out of the solid rock, which seems to have been excavated with judgment; the little hollows (*a*) (*b*) (*c*), are well contrived for holding fodder; at (*a*) two horses may feed together; at (*b*) and (*c*) one each.

Also in the area immediately surrounding Sherwood is the church of St. Mary's in Edwinstowe village which is frequently given as an alternative (but less reliable) site for the marriage of Robyn and Marian, another St. Mary's church in Blindworth village is where the traditional 'Grave Of Will Scarlet' can still be seen in the churchyard, and the Wardens Of Sherwood were based at Papplewick village which, in much later legend, was said to be the home of Allen a'Dale.

Robin Hood's Stable – Papplewick, Sherwood (SK 548517) was a possibly medieval cave cell cut into the local sandstone for use as stables and having at least one gothic arch carved inside. It was poorly illustrated and filled in for safety reasons in the 19th century thus remaining as an archaeological 'conundrum' for future generations to investigate.

Swineshead Abbey, Newark Castle & 'King John's Palace' Clipstone

On a march up the east coast King John famously lost the treasure in the Wash between King's Lynn and Newark. He pulled back to Swineshead Abbey where he drowned his sorrows on 'peaches and new cider', then he moved on to Sleaford to the west and the Bishop Of Lincoln's Castle at Newark where he died after three days unknown illness (possibly poisoning) on the 18th October 1216 aged just 48. Both the Abbey and Castle survive today as major visitor attractions.

On the way it is said that he stopped at the Three Kings Inn which has reputedly stood on the same site since 871 (a pub also named at various times the 'Harvest Home' and 'Barley Mow') and the hostelry still stands on the road to this day. Why did King John turn in-land at his greatest hour of need?

Possibly the resources and comforts of his palace at Clipstone hold the answer? The site of 'King John's Clipstone' or ' King John's Hunt' is currently being investigated and developed as a major archaeological site and visitor attraction – even though King John never made it there on his last visit if he was actually trying to reach the safety of his palace! The site was originally founded and developed by at least two other monarchs either side of the reign of King John and initial investigations have revealed a great deal of activity in a wide surrounding area. As a site this is clearly one to watch in the future.

Friar Tuck's Hermitage Fountaindale

'Friar Tuck's Hermitage' at Fountaindale is said to be the cave to which Friar Tuck had retreated just before joining forces with Robyn Hoode and his band of outlaws and it certainly resembles the type of site frequently used by hermits during the medieval period. In medieval times a stream flowed through the valley below and legend has it that Robyn fought with the feisty friar here before becoming life-long friends and allies, a similar tale to the later legend of Robyn's first meeting with Little John.

The Grave, Gate House & Priory Ruins at Kirklees

In the grounds of Kirklees House is the famous *'Grave In The Woods'* which can be said with reasonable certainty to be a fake derived from the confusions of 18th century antiquarians. This monument site is now in private ownership and visiting the remains of this grave 'folly' is no longer encouraged. In

Robin Hood's Grave Kirklees C.1870.

any case it is perhaps best to view it simply as a private tribute to Robyn Hoode erected by the antiquarians of a bygone age. Only three panes of leaded window illustrating Robyn Hoode's men remain in the nearby pub as a tiny clue to a once booming tourist trade.

According to Richard Grafton in his *'Chronicle'* of 1562, Robyn was buried beside the road *"where he used to rob and spoil those that passed that way"* and upon his grave was written *"the names of Robert Hood, William of Goldesborough, Thomas, and others . . . and at either end of the said tomb was erected a cross of stone, which is to be seen at this present time."* This is certainly the stone illustrated in the 17th century by Nathaniel Johnson and does not rule out its origin being from elsewhere "along the main road" – but we do not know from where.

Although we don't have an original surviving grave slab claimed to be that of Robyn Hoode the forester knight, we do have some fine examples of other contemporary knights and foresters tomb lids of the same period and in the same areas to compare the illustration with, in addition to possibly the original grave slab of Little John at Hathersage. Some of these include:

Melbourne Parish Church, St Michael with St Mary, Staffordshire

Without doubt this is one of the finest surviving Norman Churches in the country and is contemporary with Robyn Hoode, having a forester's tomb stone hidden in the vestry almost identical in design to that supposed to have covered Little John (and very similar to late 17th and 18th century illustrations of Robyn's tombstone). To get the feel of such original ecclesiastical buildings of Robyn's day a visit here is a must.

St John The Baptist Church, Tideswell

Cross On The End Of The Box Tomb In St John The Baptist Church Tideswell.

Has a magnificent 'open' box tomb with a carved dead body inside and a prominent forester's cross set into the altar facing end. This is probably the closest surviving tomb to that which actually covered the real burial of Robyn Hoode, as Richard Grafton records of Robyn's tomb in his *'Chronicle'* of 1569: *"Either end of the tomb was a cross of stone"*.

Parish Church Of All Saints Claverley, Diocese Of Hereford

This tiny church has the equivalent to the 'British Beaux Tapestry' painted on it's walls depicting knights of the Third Crusade in various forms of combat, and including the Templar coded 'Lilly Crucifix' (a twisty leaf and tree design) twice, as well as at least

eight Templar dedication and 'saints' crosses on various parts of the walls. The Lilly Crucifix was a secret Templar Code for the 'True Cross', sometimes has the figure of Christ depicted attached to it, and

appears on King Richard the Lion Heart's later 'Great Seal'.

While the church was certainly standing in the days of Robyn Hoode there is currently no evidence that he actually visited the site. It simply illustrates, in a very unique way, episodes and beliefs which would have been current at that time and in this particular geographic area. As a forester, knight, and servant of King Richard, the symbolism illustrated on these walls would have been very familiar to the real Robyn Hoode.

The Collegiate Church Of Saint Bartholomew, Tong, Staffordshire

This much larger church, also in the geographic area associated with Robyn Hoode, has the ruins of a Hospitaller hospital and a Templar side chapel with an altar and three painted dedication

The Collegiate Church Of Saint Bartholomew Tong Staffordshire.

crosses dating to the time of Robyn and the Third Crusade. The medieval Templar altar was found in use as a church step and has been re-sited the right side up with six fine Crusader dedication crosses now facing upwards. There is also another detailed wooden Lilly Crucifix carved on the underside of one of the medieval choir seats which in this instance shows the figure of Christ attached.

Welbeck Abbey & Imposing Georgian House

In 1199 King John granted the Upper Derwent estate (most of the Ronksley Valley) to the monks known as 'White Canons' of Welbeck Abbey perhaps in the hope of quelling the outlaws there (a similar mover tried elsewhere with Augustinian Black Cannons).

However the White Canons hated the 'liberal' Black Canons as much as the outlaws did and the outlaws and White Canons appear to have got on rather well. Maybe this is the origin of the rebellious side of Friar Tuck? It is even possible that Robyn had one of his camps in the remote valley of 'Abbey Brook' behind their Abbey here at Welbeck.

Medieval Boundary Wall Derbyshire.

Kirkstall Abbey

The closest Abbey Church to Wakefield is Kirkstall Abbey, its founder Henry de Lacy is frequently connected to Robyn Hoode, it had direct connections to Fountains Abbey where Robyn's relics ended up, it was developed within the life-time of Robyn (founded 19 May 1147), it resides within the area of Leeds (Lees), and it was formerly a Saxon church set in woodland clearings named 'Kirk-stoel' meaning simply 'Church-place'.

Being completely impartial this may be one possible *"Abbey"* site referred to by Robyn when he expresses the desire in Skelton's 1547 play to be buried *"... at Wakefield, underneath the abbey wall."* in which case the real Robyn Hoode lies buried somewhere under its walls.

Nostell Priory

However, another candidate may be Nostell Priory in the village of Wragby located between Doncaster and Wakefield. It was a 12th century Augustinian foundation with Templar connections dedicated to St Oswald supported initially by Robert de Lacy of Pontefract, Thurstan of York, William I Foliot and later by King David of Scotland in the days of Robyn Hoode. 'Aldulf' confessor to King Henry I (1100-1135) was the first known prior in about 1114.

Being completely impartial once again this may be another possible *"Abbey"* site referred to by Robyn when he expresses the desire in Skelton's 1547 play to be buried *"... at Wakefield, underneath the abbey wall."* in which case the real Robyn Hoode lies buried somewhere under its walls.

Wakefield Cathedral Of All Saints

The current Wakefield Cathedral of All Saints in the center of the old medieval town of Wakefield was always thought to stand on the site of an early Saxon church recorded in the Domesday Survey, and which was almost certainly under reconstruction in stone around the time of Robyn's death. Archaeological work below floor level in 2013 revealed the plan of a tiny original Medieval Church with several burials (formerly under carved stone lids) close to the altar end. Time and budget constraints severely limited investigation and only the upper layer could be investigated in any detail, carbon dating results however placed

the three early burials in the 12th century – close enough to confirm significant burials in the time of Robyn Hoode.

Wessex Archaeology Excavate The Top Layer Of Under-Floor Remains Wakefield Cathedral 2013. (Courtesy Of Wessex Archaeology).

No further excavation was permitted, the new floor was set in place, and the body of the real Robyn Hoode was most probably entombed again for future generations to discover.

Ironically the location of these and certainly other significant medieval burials now lie below a huge square wooden altar table in the shape of a Templar cross.

8

The Arrow & the Pen

There are a great many records surviving from the times of Robyn Hoode and they combine to form a hugely complicated picture of the relationship between leading characters in the areas Robyn inhabited. Unfortunately it is these many thousands of records that paint the most vivid picture of the world in which Robyn and his men operated here in lands north of the river Trent so we must attempt to summarize the information they contain and create some outline of the leading characters that surround and impact on Robyn's life.

It is known that King Richard sold off Scotland to raise money for his Crusades, and that he gave ownership of the lands between the river Mersey and the river Ribble to a group of Earl's and Barons creating a 'Shire' (later known as a 'Palatine County' or self-governing region) not an 'Honour' as was usual in these times. Principle in this 'land grab' would have been those families associated with the long-established regional centers of Chester, Lancaster, and York.

Prominent names here include: Meschin (Chester), Gernons (Chester), Lacy (Chester and Lancaster), Blunderville (Chester), Botiller (Warrington), Kevellioc (Chester), Glanville (Lancashire and Yorkshire), Grelly (Manchester), Venables (Derbyshire), Peveril (Derbyshire), Lyttle (Derbyshire), Ferrers (Staffordshire), Marmion (Staffordshire and Yorkshire), Foliot (Nottinghamshire), Aumale (Yorkshire), Percy (Yorkshire), Beaumont (Warrington), and Gaunt (Lancashire).

There is an actual recorded case of a meeting of ten Northern Barons and two Ecclesiastics translated in Drake's book on York 'Eboracum' (a similar gathering to those that would have been held in the cities of Chester and Lancaster).

Archbishop Thurston, whom King Stephen (1135-1154) had appointed lieutenant-governor of the north, called together the nobility and gentry of the counties, and those adjoining the city of York when King David of Scotland (1124-1153) invaded parts of England. The names recorded in this instance were: Richard prior of Hexham, William de Albermarle (Aumale), Walter de Gant (Gaunt), Robert de Brus, Robert de Mowbray, Walter Espec, Ilbert de Lacy, William de Percy, Richard de Curcy, William Fossard, and Robert de Stoutville, described as all Ancient Barons of this country.

We know that these Northern Barons held lands in what is now Lancashire, Cheshire, Cumbria, and Yorkshire up to Hadrian's Wall and a few names link directly to Robyn.

John, later King John 'Lackland', would have disapproved of such a land grab, and clearly made attempts to reverse the process in whatever ways he could when the opportunity presented itself.

After the death of King Richard, John took a particular interest in Liverpool, Halton and Frodsham (close to Chester, Stanlow, and Norton) as a controlling area for north Cheshire / south Lancashire, then turned his attention to developing coastal areas north of Lancaster, below Cumbria (Cumberland) and the Scots borders, especially in areas associated with Robyn's land ownership in later life (such as Ingleton and Plumpton Park).

It seems clear from the areas concerned that Richard had left instructions that his younger brother should stay 'south of the river Trent' in order not to antagonize the land owning Northern Barons, advice which John ignored, especially after Richard's death. This created the clash of the 'Red Team' supporting Richard to the north and west, with the 'Blue Team' supporting John in the south and east, and Robyn became the defender of this border zone on behalf of the Northern barons creating the 'Green Team'. Behind the Northern barons also rested the power of the frequently connected Scots (the 'Yellow Team'), and later the power and support of the French against King John.

A good and quite common example is the marrying of the Earls Of Chester to Scots brides. One typical good example is Robert Grelly of Manchester, grandson of the first Robert Grelly, who married the daughter of Balliol of Scotland thus forging an alliance. Robert Grelly and the Grelly family can clearly be shown to be a member of the table of Northern Barons. There are even distant Scots links in Robyn's own family background. The 'de Lacy's held land from Halifax over to the East coast and probably considered it all as their own after a deal with Richard the first. It appears that the family almost became contenders for the throne following the death of King Richard and were certainly extremely powerful nationally, with one branch holding virtually all of the Welsh marches and the other holding every-thing from the river Mersey to the Scots border.

It is clearly understandable that King John would stand against such a powerful household, and that they would respond by forming a trained militia from knights, foresters, and the newly forming class of youngermen (yeomen), to defend their border lands. Chances are their soldiers and archers were trained in areas surrounding Chester, possibly around Halton and Frodsham, where there are street and pub names including 'Robin Hoode' and evidence for a great many archery butts and military tilting grounds which would have been very familiar to Robyn's potential commander Roger 'Hell' de Lacy (fitz Eustace) and the other Northern Barons.

It appears that the sons of Nobles and Barons acted as the defending warrior force in the conflicts between Richard and John, even if only a few of those names are known when they faced the forces of King John around Lincoln and Nottingham. Little John was probably a noble's son, brother, or lesser relative, rather than a Baron himself, as was Robert Constable and the other pillars of the terrorist force which stood against John. And being a relative of the northern families ensured loyalty.

Furthermore these aristocratic and knightly households must have been the vehicle through which the tales of Robyn Hoode were sustained, performed, viewed, and developed. For example, the combined honours of de Lacy and Lancaster bridge the gap between Barnsdale and Sussex, Pontefract and de Lacy estates north of Clitheroe, Sherwood and Barnsdale, and even help explain the knowledge of, and inclusion of, Friar Tuck. These tales were written by Youngermen about Youngermen and for Youngermen, by a dedicated and developing group of royal servants.

King John effectively waged war on North Lancashire from around 1200 to 1205, savaging the areas around Halton and further north and imprisoning Roger de Lacy's brother Robert for four or five years for reasons that today are not altogether clear. King John then undertook extensive travel to and from Ireland and made visits higher up the coast in an attempt to get a foothold in North Lancashire, Cumbria, and areas surrounding the Irish Sea. It appears that the de Lacy's resisted John's efforts to gain a foothold high up on the west coast joined by Lady Dergovilla and the Scots. Eventually King John is directly responsible for the establishment of the port of Liverpool.

Meanwhile, being just north of the river Trent, the Foliot's of Jordan Castle near Centre Parks, Nottingham, were constantly under pressure from John so they turned to Chester for help! We have it in writing in the form of early charters that William Foliot was good friends and a business partner with Robert de Lacy many years before John was on the scene. They both gave land for Nostell Priory to be built (and even King David of Scotland put funds into the venture), meanwhile de Percy was feathering his bed further North and it looks like they had to write a gift and then reconfirm it, so there are two documents for each land gift which shows that there must have been an excellent functioning clerical system in those days. Each Lord or Baron,

Earl or King etc, could not possibly remember each and every 'bovate' or parcel of land they held. It was the start of what we know now as the Civil Service and I suspect at this time that Chester's Civil Service was just as good as London's, if not better.

In 1199 there is a 99% probability of a meeting in Chester of Northern Earls, Barons, Lords, etc, to discuss what happens next after King Richard's untimely death! It would be a reasonable guess that there were a few, including a 'royalist' faction saying we now have to follow King John as king no matter what, and others arguing that John was not fit to be a king, maybe going further and even claiming that the throne should be taken by one of them, possible by a de Lacy.

This would have sparked a heated debate but the older and wiser knights would have calmed the waters and suggested that nothing could be done except to keep their heads down and wait. If they waged war on John all hell would breaki loose with the north versus the south, and then the Scots and French would have come in along with the Welsh and Irish providing an opportunity to jump in and join the land grab. But worst of all yet another load of greedy young European Barons would have come over fighting for one side or the other as mercenaries and what a disaster for ruling structure and ownership that would have been! Instead I honestly believe a 'war of attrition' was devised, hence the use of forest based terrorist groups hindering John where ever they could.

However John must have known who was behind this apparent disloyalty to the crown, this being one of the reasons John went over to Ireland, and then back to Lancaster, waging war on the de Lacy's and others who opposed him. Where did this all eventually end? Well the wise old men fought with the pen and with wisdom, they slowly got enough barons together to force John to sign a major charter, the Magna Carta, laying out the laws of the land that even he must abide by. At Runnymede John finally found out exactly who was behind the attacks both by the arrow and the pen.

Jerusalem

Bring me my Bow of burning gold;
Bring me my Arrows of desire:
Bring me my Spear; O clouds unfold !
Bring me my Chariot of fire !
I will not cease from Mental Fight,
Nor shall my Sword sleep in my hand:
Till we have built Jerusalem,
In England's green and pleasant Land.
William Blake.

Appendix & List of Useful Sources

Oldest Surviving Written References (C.1300-1600)

The following list does not repeat any reference to the variant names of 'Robyn Hoode' or his possible family so far discovered in manuscripts relating to medieval legal or land matters as these have already been extensively quoted and date to the 12th and 13th century. What follow are references appearing in popular literature, poetry and chronicles.

1283: Probably the earliest written source to survive anywhere is a French pastoral play written by Adam de la Halle in around 1283 entitled *'Robin et Marion'* in which the shepherdess Marion successfully resists the advances of a knight in an attempt to stay loyal to her lover Robin. Certainly as far as the French are concerned, this places Robin and Marion together right at the start of surviving written tales.

1304: The earliest surviving dateable literary reference to Robyn Hoode so far discovered in the British Isles appears in a Latin poem written by the Prior of Alnwick. In its title William Wallace is disparagingly described as *'the Scottish Robin Hood'* and the year '1304' is written next to it in the margin. If nothing else this proves that the fame and deeds of Robyn Hoode had reached Scotland by the 13th century.

1362: Robyn Hoode appears in William Langland's *'Piers Plowman'*: *"I do not know my paternoster (prayers) perfectly as the* *priest sings it, But I know rhymes of Robin Hood and Ranulf, Earl of Chester."* Once again both rhymes had clearly become established and the two characters apparently linked in the minds of the readers.

1376: English poet John Gower has Robin and Marion taking part in rustic festivals in his lengthy moral poem *'Mirour de l'homme'* or *'Speculum Meditantis'* written in French between 1376 and 1379, and speaks out against the revels of monks with the comment that they would rather obey the rule of Robin than that of St Augustine.

1377: At some point in the 14th Century, possibly between 1377 and 1384, John Fordun, canon of Aberdeen, also briefly refers to Robyn Hoode in his *'Scottish Chronicles' ('Scotichronicon')* as *'ille famosissimus sicarius'*, *'that most celebrated murderer'*. The word *'siccarius'* from the latin *'knife'* would translate *'knife-man'*, with later modern connotations of *'cut-throat'*. When this book was revised by Walter Bower around 1440 he added: *"Then (C.1266) arose the famous murderer, Robert Hood, as well as Little John, together with their accomplices from among the disinherited, whom the foolish populace are so inordinately fond of celebrating both in tragedies and comedies, and about whom they are delighted to hear the jesters and minstrels sing above all other ballads."* (Although it is not clear if Walter Bower was referring to the actual life or spreading fame of Robyn with his use of the word *"arose"* and the date is also widely open to debate.)

1420: Andrew de Wyntoun records that Little John and Robyn Hoode were renowned in the thirteenth century in his *'Original Chronicle Of Scotland'*.

1445: Scottish writer Walter Bower records *'the most famous cutthroat Robin Hood'* as an historic figure about which much nonsense was written.

1460: The *"Polychronicon"*, a work on general history in the Eton College Library, has a late margin entry written in Latin by a monk around the year C.1460: *"Around this time* (13th Century)*, according to popular opinion, a certain outlaw named Robin Hood, with his accomplices, infested Sherwood and other law-abiding areas of England with continuous robberies."* The original text of the *'Polychronicon'* is usually ascribed to Ranulf Higden (C.1280-1364) a Benedictine monk who joined St. Werburgh's Abbey in Chester in 1299 and seems to have traveled widely across the north of England. It was translated by John of Trevisa in 1387, expanded between 1432 and 1450, and printed by Caxton in 1480.

If the original text for the *"Polychronicon"* was indeed composed in Chester around the year 1299 it represents the earliest actual historic reference to Robyn Hoode and entirely validates an early date for his life and geographic location.

1473: Sir John Paston of Norfolk mentions in a letter to his brother that he has paid a servant to act in Robyn Hoode plays and refers to *"Barnsdale"* as Robyn's base.

1475: A dramatic fragment exists of *'Robyn Hod and the Shryff off Notyngham'* in Cambridge, *Trinity College MS R.2.64 (fragment),* dated C.1475. The language used in this fragment points to an earlier date for the original material.

1500: Poet Alexander Barclay, writing just after 1500, is the first surviving English writer to record *'... some merry fytte of Maid Marian or else of Robin Hood'* showing that such material was linked together here in Britain but that possibly separate traditions still survived concerning both leading characters.

1515: Robin (and all the other associated characters) appears as the 'host' for the Maying celebrations at the court of Henry VIII in the year 1515, an event based on *'The Downfall of Robert Earl of Huntington'*.

1521: Scottish writer John Major states that Robyn (*Robertus Hudus*) was outlawed between 1193 and 1194 while Richard I was held captive in Germany in his *'History Of Greater Britain'*.

1542: Henry VIII's chief antiquarian John Leland refers to Robyn Hoode as an historical figure in his *'Collectanea'*.

1555: The Scottish Parliament prohibited any and all 'impersonations' of Robin Hood, Little John, the Abbot Of Unreason, or the Queen Of The May, in all Royal Burghs on penalty of five years imprisonment and banishment (with only slightly less severe punishments in other areas).

1557: The 'Stationer's Register' records the *"Ballett of Wakefylde and a grene"* for the year 1557-1558 and the *"Ballett of Robyn Hod"* for 1562-1563, and a 'Captain Cox' is noted as possessing 'stories' which include Robin Hood, but the contents of these works are unknown and none of these now survive.

1562: Richard Grafton claims in his *'Chronicle'* to have discovered an *"old and authentic pamphlet"* recording the life of Robyn Hoode.

The poet Drayton (1563-1631) describes the various ensigns or devices of the English Counties at the battle of Agincourt (1415) and gives to:

> *"Old Nottingham, an archer clad in green,*
> *Under a tree with his drawn bow that stood,*
> *Which in a chequered flag far off was seen,*
> *It was the picture of Robin Hood."*

Was this the former black and white chequered flag of the Templars with the figure of the famous Templar archer Robyn Hoode superimposed?

Oldest Surviving Detailed Sources (C.1400-1600)

All these surviving detailed sources are versions of printed manuscripts, the most consistent being *'A Lyttell Geste Of Robyn Hode'*, and the majority dating through the 1500'ds. *Only six surviving Robin Hood Ballads can be positively dated to before 1500* and these are:

1]. *Robin Hood And The Monk* (or: *Talking Of The Monk And Robin Hood*) = Cambridge University – Dated C.1450.

2]. *Robin Hood And Guy Of Gisbourne* = A full version survives in the *Percy Folio* (C.1650) and appears in part on the *'Dramatic Fragment'*, Trinity College, Cambridge, - Dated 1475 (or slightly earlier).

3]. *Robin Hood And The Curtal Friar* = A full version of this also survives in the *Percy Folio* (C.1650) and appears on the *'Dramatic Fragment'*, Trinity College, Cambridge, - Dated 1475 (or slightly earlier).

4]. *Robin Hood And The Potter* = The oldest complete surviving manuscript version of this has expenses detailed on one page for the marriage feast of Henry VII's daughter Margaret to James IV of Scotland in 1502 (making it slightly earlier).

5.1]. *A Geste Of Robyn Hode* = The 'A Text' (*Antwerp Copy*), Advocates Library, Edinburgh, appeared in print by C.1492-1510.

5.2 / 5.3 / 5.4 / 5.5]. *A Lyttell Geste Of Robyn Hode* = The 'B Text' (*Wynken de Worde*), University Of Cambridge Library - appeared in print C.1515. Scholars have concluded on linguistic grounds that both *'Geste'*s were probably composed around the year C.1400. The 'C, D, and E Texts' (C.1550s) are small fragments in the Bodleian Library Oxford.

5.6]. *A Mery Geste Of Robyn Hoode* = The 'F Text" (*William Copland*) C.1550, British Library (reprint of The 'B Text').

5.7]. *A Mery Jest Of Robyn Hood* = The 'G Text' (*Edward White*) after C.1560, British Library (reprint of The 'B Text').

6]. *Robin Hood: His Death* = An incomplete version in the *Percy Folio* C.1650 matches the final short account in the *'Geste'* suggesting a much earlier date for this complete tale.

Alexander Barclay makes mention of Robyn in his collection of poems entitled *'The Ship Of Follies'* written in 1508:

Yet would I gladly hear some merry fytte
Of Maid Marian, or else of Robin Hood.

Shakespeare also makes mention of Robyn in what is considered by some to be his first play (written between 1589 and 1592) *'The Two Gentlemen Of Verona'* when the character 'Valentine' is banished from Milan into the forests where outlaws want him to be their leader commenting *"By the bare scalp of Robin Hood's fat friar, This fellow were a king for our wild faction!"*

There is also a second, more specific reference in *'As You Like It'* (C.1599) where Shakespeare writes:

"They say he is already in the forest of Arden,
and a many merry men with him;
and they live like the old Robin Hood of England;
- and fleet the time carelessly,
as they did in the golden world."

 Anthony Munday produced two important plays in 1598, *'The Downfall of Robert Earl of Huntington'* and *'The Death of Robert Earl of Huntington'*, in which he clearly moves Robyn away from associations with the developing 'Maying' or May Day traditions and adds the twists of Robyn as the noble 'Earl Of Huntington' in the days of King Richard I with Marian named as Matilda, daughter of Robert fitz Walter (Robert 'son of' Walter) love interest of King John and, in the second play, Robyn is poisoned leaving Matilda to be pursued by John. Although much of Munday's information can be traced back to such works as the anonymous play *'The Troublesome Reign of King John'*, many elements appear here for the first time with their original source unknown.

Me thinks I see no ieasts (feasts) of Robin Hoode,
No merry morices (dances) of Frier Tuck,
No pleasant skippings up and downe the wodde,

No hunting songs, no coursing of the Bucke.
Pray God this play of ours may have good lucke,
And the King's Maiestie (Majesty) mislike it not.
Anthony Munday 'The Downfall of Robert Earl of Huntington' 1598.

Later Surviving Detailed Sources (C.1600-1800)

The 17th century got off to a good start for references to Robyn Hoode when Robert Cecil, 1st Earl of Salisbury and then Secretary Of State, branded Guy Fawkes and his associates *"Robin Hoods"* for sedition and treachery in the 'Gunpowder Plot' of 1605. The fact that military and legal associations have frequently been made with Robyn Hoode up to this point in time speaks volumes for the widely held opinion that he was a genuine historic character worthy of note.

The following list is loosely based on 33 ballads collected by the compiler Childs from sources up to the 18th century. However there are some he missed and a few other relevant compositions from this period, all of which have been checked against *'Robin Hood's Garland'* which survives from a publication of 1670 and contains 16 early compositions. (There is a 'Garland' entitled *'The English Archer OR Robin Hood's Garland'* which contains 27 compositions, a similar later 'Garland' which contains 28, and a Victorian version which contains 53!) The great diarist Samuel Pepys (1633-1703) and his contemporary Anthony Wood also included printed chapbooks and broadsides in their collections, thus saving many early tales from loss and destruction.

I have also attempted to group these in some semblance of

subject order, based on the general content or plot so that any stories of similar origin, message or moral can be compared by any dedicated researchers into the later material of Robyn Hoode, or compared to any new tales which may come to light in the future.

Stories concerning enmity against clergy

Robin Hood And The Curtal Friar (as in the *'Gest'*) (17th Century *'Percy Folio'*).

Robin Hood And The Bishop (Appears in early *'Garland's'*) / *Robin Hood And The Old*

Wife (Appears in the *'Foresters Manuscript'* possibly a variant of *The Bishop*).

The Knight And The Monks Of St Mary's Abbey (as in the *'Gest'*).

Robin Hood And The High Cellarer Of St Mary's Abbey (as in the *'Gest'*).

Robin Hood And The Monk (as in the *'Gest'*).

Robin Hood's Golden Prize (Appears in early *'Garland's'*) possibly a variant of:

Robin Hood And The Priests (Appears in the *'Foresters Manuscript'*).

Robin Hood And The Bishop Of Hereford (Appears in early *'Garland's'*).

Rescuing condemned men at Nottingham

Robin Hood Rescuing Three Squires (17th Century *'Percy Folio'* and early *'Garland's'*).

Robin Hood Rescuing The Widow's Three Sons From The Sheriff (Appears in early *'Garland's'*).

Robin Hood Rescuing Will Stutly (17th Century *'Percy Folio'* and in early *'Garland's'*).

Robin Hood and Will Stutly;

Shewing, How he refcued him from the Sheriff and his Men, who were going to hang him.

Tune, Robin Hood and Queen Catherine.

WHEN Robin Hood in the green wood liv'd,
  Derry, derry, down;
Under the green wood tree,
Tidings there came to him with fpeed,
  Tidings for certain;
  Hey, down, derry, derry down.

That Will. Stutly furprized was,
  And tane in Prifon lay;
Three varlets that the king had hir'd,
  Did likely him betray.

Ay, and to-morrow hang'd muft be,
  To-morrow, as foon a day;
Before they could the victory get,
  Two of 'em did Stutly flay.

When Robin Hood did hear this news,
  Lord, it did grieve him fore;
And to his merry men he faid,
  Who all together fwore,

That Will. Stutly fhould refcu'd be,
  And be brought back again;
Or elfe fhould many a gallant wight,
  For his fake their be flain.

He cloath'd himfelf in fcarlet then,
  His men were all in green;

A finer fhow throughout the world
  In no place could be feen.

Good Lord, it was a gallant fight,
  To fee them all a-row;
With ev'ry man a good broad fword,
  And eke a good yew-bow.

Forth of the green wood are they gone,
  Yea, all couragioufly;
Refolving to bring Stutly home,
  Or ev'ry man to dye.

And when they came to the caftle near,
  Wherein Will. Stutly lay;
I hold it good, faid Robin Hood,
  We here in Ambufh ftay;

And fend one forth fome News to hear,
  To yonder palmer fair,
That ftands under the caftle-wall;
  Some news he may declare.

With that fteps forth a brave young man,
  Which was of courage bold;
Thus he did fay to the old man,
  I pray thee, Palmer old,

Tell me, if that thou rightly ken,
  When mall Will. Stutly dye?

Who is one of bold Robin's men,
  And be doth prifoner lye,

Alas, alas, the palmer faid,
  And for ever woe is me!
Will Stutly hang'd will be this day,
  On yonder gallows tree.

O had his noble mafter known,
  He would fome fuccour fend;
A few of his bold yeomen fend,
  Full foon would fetch him hence.

Ay, that is true the young man faid;
  Ay, that is true, faid he;
Or if they were near to this place,
  They foon would fet him free.

But, fare thee well, thou good old man;
  Farewel, and thanks to thee;
If Stutly hang'd be this day,
  Reveng'd his death will be.

No fooner he was from the palmer gone,
  But the gates were open'd wide,
And out of the caftle Will. Stutly came,
  Guarded on every fide.

When he was forth from the caftle came,
  And faw no help was nigh:
Thus he did fay unto the fheriff,
  Thus he faid gallantly:

Now facing that I needs mull dye,
  Grant me one boon, faid he;
For my noble mafter ne'er had man,
  That yet was hang'd on tree:

Give me a fword all in my hand,
  And let me be unbound,
And with thee and thy men I'll fight,
  Till I lie dead on the ground.

But this defire he would not grant,
  His wifhes were in vain;
For the fheriff fwore, he hang'd fhould be,
  And not for the wood be flain.

Do but unbind my hands, he fays,
  I will no weapon crave;
And if I hanged be this day,
  Damnation let me have.

O no, no, no, the fheriff faid,
  Thou fhalt on gallows dye;
Ay, and fo fhall thy mafter too,
  If ever he come it fie.

O daftard coward, Stutly cries,
  Faint hearted, peafant flave!
If ever my mafter do thee meet,
  Thou fhalt thy payment have.

My noble mafter the doth fcorn,
  And all thy cowardly crew;
Such filly imps unable are
  Bold Robin to fubdue.

But when he was to the gallows gone,
  And ready to bid adieu;
Out of a bufh fteps little John,
  And good Will Scutly to:

I pray thee Will. before thou die,
  Of thy dear friends take leave;
I needs mull borrow him a while,
  How fay you, mafter fheriff?

Now, as I live, the fheriff faid,
  That varlet will I know:
Some fturdy rebel is that fame,
  Therefore let him not go.

Then little John, moft haftily,
  Away cut Stutly's bands,
And from one of the fheriff's men
  A fword twitch'd from his hand:

Here Will. Scutly, take thou this fame;
  Thou can't it better fway;
And here defend thy felf a while,
  For aid will come ftraitway.

And there they turn'd them back to back,
  In the midft of them that day,
Till Robin Hood approached near,
  With many an archer gay.

With that, an arrow from them free;
  I wift, from Robin Hood:
Make hafte, make hafte, the fheriff he faid,
  Make hafte, for it is not good.

The fheriff is gone; his deughny men
  Thought it no boot to ftay;
But, as their mafter had them taught,
  They run full faft away.

O ftay, O ftay, Will. Scutly faid;
  Take leave, ere you depart;
You ne'er will catch bold Robin Hood,
  Unlefs you dare him meet.

O ill betide you, faid Robin Hood,
  That you fo foon are gone;
My fword may in the fcabbard reft,
  For here our work is done.

I little thought, Will. Scutly faid,
  When I came to this place,
For to have met with little John,
  Or have feen my mafter's face.

Thus Scutly he was at liberty fet,
  And fafe brought from his foe;
O thanks, O thanks to my mafter,
  Since here it was not fo.

And once again, my fellows dear,
  Derry, derry, down;
We fhall in the green woods meet;
  Where we fhall make our bow ftring twang,
  Mufick for us moft fweet;
  Hey down, derry, derry down.

Tales of heroic archery and royalty

Robin Hood Goes Fishing / *Robin Hood's Fishing* / *Robin Hood's Preferment* /
  The Noble Fisherman (Best version survives in the *'Foresters Manuscript'*).
Robin Hood And The King (as in the *'Gest'*).
King Richard And Robin Hood (Appears in early *'Garland's'*).
Robin Hood's Court Life And His Return To The Forest (as in the *'Gest'*).
Robin Hood And Queen Catherine (17th Century *'Percy Folio'* and in early *'Garland's'*).
Robin Hood's Progress To Nottingham (Appears in early *'Garland's'*).
Robin Hood, Little John, And The Sheriff (as in the *'Gest'* / *'Foresters Manuscript'*) / *The*
  Shooting Match At Nottingham (as in the *'Gest'*) / *(Robin Hood And) The Golden Arrow*
  (Appears in early *'Garland's'*).
Robin Hood's Chase (Sequel to *'Queen Catherine'* in which King Henry chases Robin through the northern counties only to return empty handed to London. Appears in early *'Garland's'*).

Stories concerning disguise and deception

Robin Hood And Guy Of Gisburne (as in the *'Gest'*) (17th Century *'Percy Folio'*).
The King's Disguise And Friendship With Robin Hood (as in the *'Gest'*).
Robin Hood And The Potter (as in the *'Gest'*).
Robin Hood And The Beggar: Pt.1. Robin Hood Fights With The Beggar And Changes Clothes With Him, Pt.2. Robin Hood Saves Three Deer Stealers From Being Hanged (Appears in early *'Garland's'*).

Renowned ROBIN HOOD: Or, his Archery truly related, in his Exploits before Queen Catherine.

GOLD ta'en from the King's Harbingers,
  Down, a down, a dou;
As seldom hath been ta'en, *down, &c.*
And carried by bold Robin Hood,
  for a Present to the Queen.
If that I live one Year to an end,
  thou dull Queen Catherine say,
Bold Robin Hood, I will be thy friend,
  and all my Yeomen gay.
The Queen is to her Chamber gone,
  as fast as she could win,
She calls unto her lovely Page,
  his name was Richard Partington.
Come thou hither to me thou lovely Page,
  come thou hither to me;
For thou must post to Nottingham,
  as fast as thou canst thee,
And as thou goest to Nottingham,
  search all these English woods,
Enquire of one good Yeoman or another,
  that can tell thee of Robin Hood.
Sometimes he went, sometimes he ran,
  as fast as he could win,
...

there he took up his Inn.
He call'd for a bottle of Rhenish Wine,
  and drank a health to the Queen;
Willing he might now speedily
  find out jolly Robin.
There sat a Yeoman by his side,
  we'll said, sweet Page tell me,
What is thy business or thy cause,
  so far in the North Country?
This is my business and my cause,
  Sir, I'll tell it you for good,
To enquire of one good Yeoman or another,
  to tell me of Robin Hood.
I'll tell thee of Robin Hood,
  And I will shew thee bold Robin Hood,
  and all his Yeomen gay,
When that he came to Robin Hood's Place,
  Queen Catherine she doth say,
Ho greets you well by me,
She bids you post to fair London Court,
  not fearing any thing,
For there shall be a little Sport,

and she hath sent you her Ring,
Robin Hood took his Mantle from his Back,
  it was of Lincoln Green,
And sent it by this lovely Page,
  for a Present to the Queen.
In Summer-Time when Leaves grow Green,
  it was a seemly Sight to see,
How Robin Hood had dreft himself,
  and all his Yeomandree;
He clothed his Men in Lincoln Green,
  himself in Scarlet Red,
Black Hats, white Feathers all alike,
  now bold Robin Hood is rid.
And when he came to London Court,
  he fell down on his Knee,
Thou art welcome, Locksly, said the Queen,
  and so is all thy good Yeomandree.
Come hither, Tepas, said the King,
  flow heater after me;
Come measure me out with this Line,
  show long our Mark must be.
What is the wager? said the Queen,
  that thou art willing to lay;
Three Hundred Tun of Rhenish Wine,
  three Hundred Tun of Beer,
Three Hundred of the fattest Harts,
  that run on Dallon Lee;
That's a Princely Wager, said the Queen,
  betwixt your Grace and me.
With that bespoke one Clifton then,
  full quickly and full foon,
Measure no Mark for us, most Sovereign Liege,
  we'll shoot at Sun and Moon.
Full fifteen Score your Mark shall be,
  full fifteen Score fet ye,
I'll lay my Bow, said Clifton then,
  I'll cleave the Willow-Wand.
With that the King's Archers led about,
  till it was three or none;
With that the Ladies began to shout,
  Madam your Grace is gone.
A Boon, a Boon, Queen Catherine cries,
  I crave it on my Knee;
Is there ever a Knight of your Privy-Council,
  of Queen Catherine's Side will be?
Come hither to me, Sir Richard Lee,
  thou art a Knight full good;
For I do know thy Pedigree,
  thou sprung'st from Gower's Blood.
Come hither to me, thou Bishop of Hereford-shire,
  for a noble Priest was he;
By my Silver Mitre, said the Bishop then,
  I'll not bet one Penny.
The King had Archers all his own,
  full ready and full right,
And there be strange every one,
  no Man knows what they height.
What wilt thou bet? said Robin Hood,
  you fee our Queen's the work;

By my Silver Mitre, said the Bishop,
  all the Money within my Purse.
What is in thy Purse? said Robin Hood,
  throw it out on the Ground;
Ninety nine Angels said the Bishop,
  it's near an Hundred Pound,
Robin Hood took his Bag from his Side,
  and threw it on the Green,
Will Scadlock then went smiling away,
  I know who this Money must win,
With that the King's Archers led about,
  while it was three to three;
With that the Ladies gave a shout,
  Woodcock, beware thy Knee.
It is three to three now, said the King,
  the next three pays for all;
Robin Hood went and whisper'd the Queen,
  the King's Part shall be but small.
Then Robin Hood did keep about,
  he shot it under Hand;
And Clifton with a bearing Bow,
  he clove the Willow-Wand.
And little Midge the Miller's Son,
  he shot not much the worse;
He shot within a Finger of the Prick,
  now, Bishop, beware thy Purse.
A Boon, a Boon, Queen Catherine cries,
  I crave it on my bare Knee;
That you will angry be with none,
  that is of my Party.
They shall have forty Days to come,
  and forty Days to go,
And three times forty to sport and play,
  then welcome Friend or Foe.
Thou art welcome Robin Hood, said the Queen,
  and so is Little John,
And so is Midge the Miller's Son;
  thrice welcome every One.
Is this Robin Hood? the King then said,
  for it was told to me, that bold Robin Hood
  was in the Palace Gate,
Is this Robin Hood? quoth the Bishop then,
  for far in the North Country,
Had I known it had been that bold Outlaw,
  as it seems well to be;
I would not have bet one Penny.
But took him now so soon I might,
  and bound me fast to a Tree,
And made me fing a Mass, God-wot,
  to him and his Yeomandree,
What, and if I did, says Robin Hood,
  that Mass it was full fain;
For Recompence of that, he says,
  here's half thy Gold again.
Now nay, now nay, says Little John,
  Master, that may not be,
We muft give Gifts to the King's Officers,
  that Gold will serve thee and me.

LONDON: Printed by L. How in Petticoat Lane.

Tales including 'Gamwell'

Robin Hood Newly Reviv'd.
The Bold Pedlar And Robin Hood.
Robin Hood And The Prince Of Aragon.
Robin Hood's Birth, Breeding, Valor And Marriage.

Other tales of Robyn Hoode include

Robin Hood And The Poor Knight (as in the *'Gest'*).
Robin Hood And Little John (Appears in early *'Garland's*).
Robin Hood And The Pinder Of Wakefield / The Jolly Pinder Of Wakefield, With Robin
 Hood, Scarlet, And Little John (17th Century *'Percy Folio'* and in early *'Garland's*).
Robin Hood And The Ranger (Appears in early *'Garland's*).
Little John a'Begging / Little John And The Four Beggars (Appears in early *'Garland's*).
Robin Hood And The Pedlars.
Robin Hood And The Valiant Knight (Appears in early *'Garland's*).
Robin Hood And Allen a'Dale (Appears in early *'Garland's*).
Robin Hood And The Butcher (17th Century *'Percy Folio'* and in early *'Garland's*).
Robin Hood (His Three Men,) And The Beggar (as in the *'Gest'*).
Robin Hood And The Tinker (Appears in early *'Garland's*).
Robin Hood And The Tanner (Appears in early *'Garland's*).
Robin Hood And The Fisherman (Appears in early *'Garland's*).
Robin Hood And The Shepherd (Appears in early *'Garland's*).
Robin Hood's Delight (Appears in early *'Garland's*).
Robin Hood And The Foresters (Appears in the *'Foresters Manuscript'*)
Robin Hood's Progress To Nottingham (Similar to above & appears in early *'Garland's*).
Robin Hood And Maid Marian (Appears in early *'Garland's /*

Robin Hoods Chace,

Or, *A merry* Progress between *Robin Hood* and King Henry.

Tune——*Robin Hood* and the *Beggar.*

COME, you Gallants all, to you I call,
Hark a little, listen, and attend,
that are now in this Place,
For a Song I will sing of Henry our King,
how he did bold Robin Hood chace.

Queen Katherine she then a match did make,
as plainly doth appear;
For three hundred Tun of good Red Wine,
and three hundred Tun of Beer.

But she had her Archers to seek.
with their Bows and Arrows so good,
But her mind it was bent, with a full intent,
to send for bold Robin Hood.

But when bold Robin Hood he came there,
Queen Katherine she did say,
Thou art welcome Locksly unto me,
and thou on my part must be.

If I miss the Mark, be it light or dark,
and all my Yeoman gay,
For a Match of Shooting I have made,
then hanged will I be.

But when the Game was to be play'd,
Bold Robin Hood won it with a Grace;
But after the King was angry with him,
and vowed he would him chafe.

What tho' his Pardon granted was,
while he with them did stay,
But yet the King was vex'd with him,
when he was gone away.

Soon after the King from Court did hie,
in a furious angry mood,
And often enquireth both far and near,
after bold Robin Hood.

But when the King to Nottingham came,
bold Robin Hood was in the Wood:
O come, said he, and let me fee
who can find bold Robin Hood.

But when bold Robin Hood he did hear
the King had him in chace;
Then said Little John, 'tis time to be gone,
and go to some other Place.

Then away they went from merry Sherwood,
and went strait to Newcastle Town,
And there he flay'd hours two or three,
and then he for Berwick was gone.

Yet jolly Robin he puff along,
and into Yorkshire did hie,
And there he flay'd hours two or three,
but could not him come nigh.

When the King he did fee how Robin Hood did flee,
he was vexed wondrous fore;
With a hoop and a hollow he vowed to follow,
and take him, or never give o'er.

Come, now let's away, said Little John,
let any Man follow that dare;
To Carlisle we'll be with our Company,
and so then to Lancaſt e

From Lancaster then to Chester they went,
and so did good King Henry;
But Robin went away for he durst not stay,
for fear of some Treachery.

Says Robin, come let us to London go,
to see our noble Queen's face;
It may be the wants our company,
which makes the King us to chace.

When Robin he came Queen Katherine before,
he fell upon his Knee,
May it pleafe your Grace, I am come to this plac
to speak with King Henry.

Queen Katherine she anfwer'd bold Robin again
the King is gone to merry Sherwood,
And when he went away to me he faid,
he would go and feek Robin Hood.

Then fare you well, my gracious Queen,
for to Sherwood I will me hie apace;
For fain I would fee what his do have with me,
if I could but meet with his Grace.

But when King Henry he came home,
full weary and vexed in mind;
And that he did hear Robin had been there,
he blamed Dame Fortune unkind.

You're welcome home, Queen Katherine cry'd,
Henry, my Sovereign Liege;
Bold Robin Hood, the Archer good,
your Perfon hath been to feek.

A boon, a boon, Queen Katherine cry'd,
I beg, it here of your Grace,
To pardon his Life, and feek not ſtrife,
and so ends Robin Hood's Chace.

London: Printed by L. How in Petticoat-lane

'Foresters Manuscript').

Robin Hood And The Stranger: Pt.1. Robin Hood And Will Scarlet, Pt.2. The Encounter With The Giants (Appears in early *'Garland's* and also combined as one story called *Robin Hood Newly Revived*).

Robin Hood's Death (17th Century *'Percy Folio'*) / *Robin Hood's Death And Burial* (Appears in early *'Garland's*).

Robin Hood's Birth, Breeding, Valour, And Marriage (Appears in early *'Garland's*).

Other tales of Robyn Hoode beyond any published 'Garland' compositions include

The Rival Archers (A love song from Jones's *'Musical Dream'* published 1606).

A True Tale Of Robin Hood (A version by Martin Parker published 1632).

Robin Whood Turned Hermit (Pub.1735. Missing from Childs list).

The Old Wife / The Butcher / The Pinder (V1) / The Bride / The Sheriffe / The King – all appear in the *'Foresters Manuscript'*, an un-published *'Garland'* with significant differences from previously known versions, and this collection of 22 Robin Hood Ballads (actually 21 as *The Pinder* appears twice) C.1660-1670 contains probably the best versions of *Robin Hoods Fishing* and *Robin Hood and Queen Catherin*.

Later tales containing some early material

Robin Hood's Garland: The Pedigree, Education, And Marriage Of Robin Hood With
  Clorinda, Queen Of Tutbury-Feast (Author unknown and published in 1760).

Robin Hood And The Scotchman.

An Adventure In Sherwood Forest.

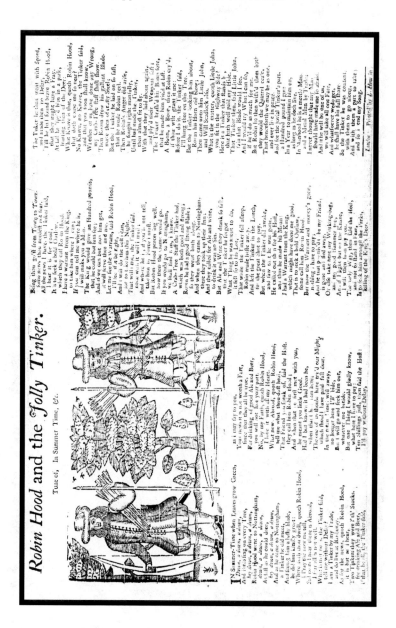

The Death Of Robin Hood.
The Rival Archers.
Robin Hood's Leap.
Robin Hood And The Duke Of Lancaster.

Robin Hood and the Shepherd:

Shewing how Robin Hood, Little John, and the Shepherd fought a fore Combat.

Tune——Robin Hood and Queen Catherine.

ALL Gentlemen and Yeomen good,
Down, a down, a Down,
I wish you to draw near;
For a Story of bold Robin Hood,
unto you I will declare;
Down, a down, a down:

As Robin Hood walk'd the Forest along,
some Pastime for to spy,
There was he aware of a Jolly Shepherd,
that on the Ground did lie.

Arise, arise, said jolly Robin,
and now come let me see,
What is in thy bag and thy bottle I say,
come, tell it unto me.

What's that to thee, thou proud Fellow:
tell me as I do stand;
What hast thou to do with my bottle and bag;
let me see thy command.

My Sword that hangeth by my side,
is my command, I know;
Come, let me taste of thy bottle,
or it may breed thee woe.

The devil a drop, thou proud Fellow,
of my bottle thou shalt see,
Untill thy Valour here be tryed,
whether thou wilt fight or flee.

What shall we fight for? said Robin Hood,
come tell it soon unto me:
Here's twenty Pounds in good red Gold,
win it and take it thee.

The Shepherd stood all in amaze,
and knew not what to say:
I have no money thou proud Fellow,
but bottle and bag I'll lay.

I am content thou Shepherd Swain,
fling them down on the Ground:
But it will breed the mickle pain,
to win my Twenty Pound.

Come draw thy Sword, thou proud Fellow,
thou standst too long to prate;
This Hook of mine shall let thee know,
a Coward I do hate.

So they fell to it full hard and sore,
it was on a Summer's day;
From Ten 'till four in the Afternoon,
the Shepherd held him in play.

Robin's Buckler prov'd his chief defence,
and fav'd him many a bang:
For every blow the Shepherd gave,
made Robin's Sword cry twang.

Many a sturdy blow the Shepherd gave,
and that bold Robin found;
'Till the blood ran tricking from his head,
then he fell to the Ground.

Arise, arise, thou proud Fellow,
and thou shalt have fair play,
If thou wilt yield before thou go,
that I have won the Day.

A boon, a boon, cry'd bold Robin,
if that a Man thou be,
Then let me take my Bugle Horn,
and blow out thrice three.

Then said the Shepherd to bold Robin,
to that I will agree;
For if thou shouldst blow 'till To-morrow morn,
I scorn one Foot to flee.

Then Robin he set his Horn to his mouth,
and he blew with might and main,
Untill he espy'd Little John
come tripping over the Plain.

Who is Yonder thou proud Fellow,
that comes down Yonder Hill?
It is Little John, bold Robin Hood's Man,
shall fight with thee thy fill.

What is the matter said Little John,
Master, come tell unto me?
My Case is bad, said Robin Hood,
for the Shepherd hath conquer'd me.

I am glad of that, cries Little John,
Shepherd turn thou to me;
For a bout with thee I mean to have,
either come fight or flee.

With all my Heart thou proud Fellow,
for it shall never be said,
That a Shepherds Hook at thy sturdy look,
will one Jot be dismay'd.

So they fell to it full hard and fore,
striving for Victory;
I will know, said John, e'er we give o'er,
whether thou wilt fight or fly.

The Shepherd gave John a sturdy blow,
with the Hook under his Chin;
Beshrew thy Heart, said Little John,
thou bately dost begin.

Nay that is nothing said the Shepherd,
Either yield to me the Day,
Or I will bang thy back and sides,
before thou goest thy way.

What dost thou think thou proud Fellow,
that thou canst conquer me?
Nay, then thou halt know before thou go,
I'll fight before I'll flee.

Again the Shepherd laid on him,
the Shepherd he begun,
Hold thy hand, cry'd jolly Robin,
I will yield the Wager won.

With all my Heart said Little John,
to that I will agree;
For he is the Flower of Shepherd Swains
the like I ne'er did fee.

Thus have you heard of Robin Hood,
also of Little John,
How a Shepherd Swain did conquer them,
the like was never known.

Robin Hood and Allen-a-Dale:

Or the manner of *Robin Hood's* refcuing a young Lady from an Old Knight, and reftoring her to *Allen-a-Dale* her former Love.

Tune of, Robin Hood in the Green Wood.

COME liften to me, you Gallants fo free,
All you that love Mirth for to hear,
And I will tell you of a bold Outlaw,
That lived in Nottinghamfhire.

As Robin Hood in the Forreft ftood,
all under the green Wood Tree,
There was he aware of a brave young Man,
as fine as fine might be.

The Younglter was clothed in Scarlet red,
in Scarlet fine and gay,
And he did frisk it over the plain,
and chaunted a Round-d-lay.

As Robin Hood next Morning ftood,
amongft the Leaves fo gay,
There did he fpy the fame young Man,
come drooping along the Way.

The Scarlet he wore the Day before,
it was clean caft away;
And every Step he fetch'd a Sigh,
alack and a well-a-day.

Then ftepped forth brave Little John,
and Midge the Miller's Son,
Which made the young Man bend his Bow,
when as he faw them come.

Stand off, ftand off, the young man faid,
What is your Will with me?
You muft come before our Mafter ftrait,
under jon green Wood Tree.

And when he came bold Robin before,
Robin afk'd him courteoufly,
O haft thou any Money to fpare
for my merry Men and me?

I have no Money, the young Man faid,
but five fhillings and a Ring;
And that I have kept thefe Seven long years,
to have it at my Wedding.

Yefterday I fhould have married a Maid,
but fhe was ta'en from me,
And chofen to be an old Knight's Delight,
whereby my poor Heart is flain.

What is thy Name, then faid Robin Hood,
come tell me without any fail?
By the Faith of my Body, then faid the young Man,
my Name it is Allen a Dale.

What wilt thou give me, faid Robin Hood,
in ready Gold or Fee,
To help thee to thy true Love again,
and deliver her unto thee?

I have no Money, than quoth the young Man,
no ready Gold or Fee,
But I will fwear upon a Book,
thy true Servant to be.

How many Miles is it to thy true Love,
come, tell me without any Guile?
By the Faith of my Body, then faid the young Man,
it is but five little Mile.

Then Robin he hafted over the plain,
he did neither ftint nor lin,
Until he came unto the Church,
Where Allen fhould keep his Wedding.

What doft thou here, the Bifhop then faid,
I prithee now tell unto me?

I am a bold Harper, quoth Robin Hood,
and the beft in the North Country.

O welcome, O welcome, the Bifhop then faid,
that Mufick beft pleafeth me:
You fhall have no Mufick quoth Robin Hood,
till the Bride and the Bridegroom I fee.

With that came in a wealthy Knight,
who was both grave and old;
And after him a finikin Lafs,
did fhine like the glittering Gold.

This is not a fit match, quoth bold Robin Hood,
that you do feem to make here;
For fince we are come to the Church,
the Bride fhall chufe her own Dear.

Then Robin Hood put his horn to his mouth,
and blew Blafts two or three;
Then Four and Twenty Bowmen bold,
came leaping over the Lee.

And when they came into the Church-Yard,
marching all on a row;
The firft Man was Allen a Dale,
to give bold Robin his Bow.

This is thy true Love, Robin he faid,
Young, Allen, as I hear fay;
And you fhall be married at the fame time,
before we depart away.

That fhall not be the Bifhop he faid;
for thy word fh. II not ftand;
They fhall be three times afk'd in the Church,
as the Law is of our Land.

Robin Hood pull'd off the Bifhop's Coat,
and put it upon Little John,
By the Faith of my Body, then Robin ha faid,
this Cloth doth make thee a Man.

When Little John went to the Quoir,
the People began to laugh;
He afk'd them feven times in the Church,
left three times fhould not be enough.

Who gives this Maid? faid Little John,
quoth Robin Hood that do I;
And he that doth take her from Allen a Dale,
full dearly fhall her buy.

And thus having ended this merry Wedding,
the Bride the look'd like a Queen;
And fo they return'd in the merry Green wood,
amongft the Leaves fo green.

The Pedigree, Education, and Marriage of *Robin Hood*, with *Clorinda*, Queen of *Titbury* Feast.

Suppos'd to be related by the FIDLER, who play'd at their WEDDING.

The Dieulacres Chronicle (fol.139r.) Contains The Story Of Earl Ranulf's Dream Shown Here In The Right Hand Column.

The 'Ballad Of Ranulf, Earl Of Chester' or 'Lord Randal' to which William Langland refers in 'Piers Plowman' C.1362.

Given the direct and very early connections made between Robyn and Earl Ranulf of Chester, it seems appropriate to add any information regarding the reference in *'Piers Plowman'* to the other ballads then in circulation regarding Earl Ranulf. One ballad stands out and has survived to our time.

It has been suggested that the activities of 'Ranulf, Earl of Chester' form the basis of the well known ballad *'Lord Randal'* which contains the lines: *"I fear you are poisoned, Lord Randall, my son."* The legend then goes on to say that Ranulf went to Hell, escaped, then visited his grandson and founded an abbey renowned for its mayhem.

According to the legend the Earl was visited on his death-bed by demons to accuse him of his sins and he was condemned to Hell, but, because of the incessant howling of the dogs while he was there, the Prince of Hell ordered that he should be expelled *"... for no greater enemy of theirs than Earl Randle had ever entered the infernal dominions."* But old Ranulf isn't finished and the story goes on to say that he appeared to his grandson Ranulf de Blundeville in a vision and commanded him to found a Cistercian Abbey near Leek at a place called 'Cholpesdale' on the site of a former chapel of St. Mary the

Seal Of Dieulacres Abbey
C.1530.

Virgin.

When the younger Ranulf de Blundeville tells his new wife Clemencia about this vision of his grandfather and the proposed foundation she exclaims in Norman French *"Deux encres or Dieu L'encres !"* – *"May God grant it increase!"* – hence the name of the place then being known as 'Dieulacres'.

Unfortunately this new abbey gained a bad reputation for the Abbot maintained an 'armed band' and his power over the nearby town of Leek in

Staffordshire was absolute. He erected gallows in Market Street and was legally authorized to hang anyone he pleased, the only stipulation of this law being that he had to give 48 hours notice to the person concerned!

A royal commission in 1379 noted that the then Abbot of Dieulacres, in order to control the area, had *"... used his armed*

men to do all the mischief they could to the people in the county of Stafford, that they have lain in wait for them, assaulted, maimed, and killed some, and driven others from place to place ..." In 1380 the abbot himself was arrested

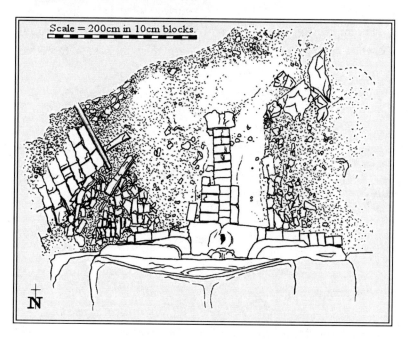

CWP Archaeology Excavated Ladydale Well In 2000 Locating The Earl's Way And Erlier Well Structure (Left Side of Plan).

and imprisoned following an incident during which a John de Wharton was beheaded by order of the Abbot, but the Abbot was soon pardoned and released. In subsequent years members of the Dieulacres community were accused of theft and the Abbot criticized for appearing to protect them. There were also numerous lawsuits.

Like so many the abbey was surrendered in 1538 putting an end to 400 years of mayhem brought about (supposedly) by the evil *'spirit of Ranulf'* and, in July 2000, an archaeological excavation and restoration of Ladydale Well in Leek established this as the most probable site of the original well, St. Mary Chapel, and 'Viam Comitis' of C.1200 (the 'High Earl's Way' medieval highway) where Ranulf de Blundeville first shared his vision with Clemencia. There has never been any evidence found for a previous chapel on the actual current site of the abbey ruins.

The monks of Dieulacres had been relocated from Poulton in Cheshire, just outside Chester, where they had been forced to retreat after the destruction of their original abbey at Stanlow Point on the River Mersey by severe storms. The remains of Stanlow Abbey still contain the bodies of at least two de Lacy's, one of them possibly the commander of Robyn Hoode and his forces, and has never been satisfactorily excavated.

The following words were carved on a wall inside the now ruined Dieulacres abbey:

"Alas, here in the wall,
enclosed beneath hard marble,
lies the heart of the Earl,
who exceeded all in daring.
O' Christ the Son of God in whom all things have their being,
do not shut the sacred gates of Heaven to Ranulph."

Hopefully, by this time, Ranulf has finally made it into heaven.

Chronos Books is a historical non-fiction imprint. Chronos publishes real history for real people; bringing to life historical people, places and events in an imaginative, easy-to-digest and accessible way. We want writers of historical books, from ancient times to the Second World War, that will add to our understanding of people and events rather than being a dry textbook; history that passes on its stories to a generation of new readers.